Beating the Street

Also by the author

Horse Sense: A New and Rigorous Application
of Mathematical Methods
to Successful Betting at the Track

BEATING THE STREET

How to Make More Money in the Stock Market

by BURTON P. FABRICAND

DAVID McKAY COMPANY, INC.
New York

BEATING THE STREET

Library of Congress Catalog Card Number: 71-79503
MANUFACTURED IN THE UNITED STATES OF AMERICA
VAN REES PRESS • NEW YORK

For

Pru, Nicki, and Lori

PREFACE

ON July 16, 1964, I bought Westinghouse Electric common stock at the opening of the stock market. Many other people had the same idea, for the opening was delayed because of a substantial influx of buy orders. Westinghouse opened a point higher at 32¼ and continued upward for the next year, more than doubling in price. For me this purchase represented the culmination of fifteen years in the stock market, and in that time I saw my original $1000 investment grow to more than $100,000.

In 1950, I had made a most fortunate decision. I cashed in some $1000 in war bonds and invested the money in common stocks, because, at the time, I felt that the stock market was very low and would go up, and that I probably would do better with my money in stocks. However, I was quite unprepared for how much better I did do.

Now, I do not consider myself particularly lucky. Many other people probably bought and sold the same stocks and did at least as well. And I certainly do not claim any special knowledge or ability to predict the future. How was it possible, then, for a rank novice among the wolves of Wall Street to accumulate such a sum? How is it possible that most other people I know make money in stocks?

This book describes my researches, actions, and thoughts about the stock market, and also about its very significant relationship to all else that goes on in the world. My findings can be summed up very simply. *You cannot afford not to be in the stock market.* A failure to own stocks means that you are not getting your fair share of the country's wealth. On balance, almost all investors make money. Much too much has been made of the riskiness of common stocks. True, some people do lose money. But most of them probably lose because they are unknowingly doing the wrong things. This book should help such investors, and enable them to do better than most.

At the present time, I advise many friends and relatives on the handling of their portfolios, whose value adds up to millions of dollars. My recommendations are made in accordance with the principles set forth in this book. Thus far, everybody has done very well indeed. This confirmation of the practical worth of my ideas is very gratifying.

I have benefited from talking to many people. First of all there is my father, Mr. I. K. Fabricand, who introduced me to the fascinating game of investing. His long experience in Wall Street as customer's man, bond dealer, and founder of the municipal bond firm of Fabricand & Co. has been invaluable. Dr. Sydney Meshkov and Dr. Julian Stone have contributed stimulating discussions. Much of the material in Chapter XI was taken from the notes of my longtime friend, the late Joseph E. North, with the permission and encouragement of his widow, Heather North. I am also indebted to my colleague, Mr. Paul Bodzin of the investment firm of Pyne, Kendall, and Hollister, for suggesting the title of the book. And finally, I would like to thank Irene Fiore for illustrations appearing in the book.

CONTENTS

CONTENTS

Beating the Street

CHAPTER I

PROBABILITY AND MONEY

The gods did not reveal from the beginning
All things to us; but in the course of time
Through seeking, men find that which is the better.

But as for certain truth, no man has known it,
Nor will he know it; neither of the gods,
Nor yet of all the things of which I speak.
And even if by chance he were to utter
The final truth, he would himself not know it;
For all is but a woven web of guesses.

XENOPHENES

GAMES of chance divide naturally into two groups. In the first group, *all* players are more likely to win than lose. I will call such games "favorable." Savings accounts, bonds, and, as we shall see, common stock investments are examples of "favorable" games. In games of the second group, which I shall term "unfavorable," all players are almost certain to lose everything they risk if they continue to play indefinitely. Horse betting, casino games, sweepstakes, and the numbers are examples of "unfavorable" games. The public, in its great wisdom, intuitively thinks about these two groups in a less technical manner, which, nonetheless, reflects the sharp difference between them. Favorable games are considered quite respectable, while unfavorable games have a taint of illegality and immorality about them, even though many now receive government sanction.

I use "game" in its broadest sense, meaning any activity in which blind chance plays a part in the outcome. Since nothing is certain but death and taxes, an element of risk enters into everything we do, and everything we do, therefore, may be thought of in terms of some appropriate game of chance. Society's great technological successes have led many of us to play down the role of chance in human affairs. But knowledge only increases our chances of success; it does not guarantee certainty. J. B. S. Haldane wrote, "The world is not only queerer than we imagine, but queerer than we can imagine."

The study of chance is the key to this book. We are going to learn how to make a lot of money in the stock market, and we are going to do it by studying games of chance, first the simpler games, then the more complicated pari-mutuel games, and finally, the stock market itself.

Anyone under the illusion that there is a simple recipe for making a lot of money, one that can be learned in a few minutes, should dispel that illusion right now. Never forget that many very smart people constantly try to get rich and fail. If there were a sure and easy method of becoming rich, all of us would be millionaires. But the problem of making money is not like the kind of fake problems we are given in school. There we are given certain facts, and from these certain conclusions follow in a reasonable manner. Order prevails. Each step is dictated by the previous step until the solution is found. Real life is hardly like that. As an example, take what happened to my friend Charlie. Charlie was very proud of his physical strength and each day performed all sorts of exercises to keep in trim. Once at a party he met some fellow who bet that he could crush a beer can flat in one hand. A good deal of money was put up. A beer can was produced, and Charlie and a number of others tried, but nobody could put more than a small dent in it. The fellow took the can and immediately crushed it flat. Well, Charlie was quite chagrined about this and decided to do something about it. For five years, he struggled through a rigorous training program designed to strengthen his hands. Each year he got stronger and was able to dent a beer can a little more. Finally, he too could crush it flat. His new prowess pleased him immensely, and he took every opportunity to demonstrate it. Just about then, I found some information in the financial pages which rather shocked poor Charlie. It seems that during the five years of his training program, the amount of steel used in beer cans had been progressively decreased: present-day beer cans were not nearly as strong as before. Charlie stoutly maintained he could crush an old beer can, too, but many of us were not so sure.

A simple story, but one that is basically similar to the problems we all face. A young lady marries her Prince Charming and expects to live happily ever after. But the day the honeymoon ends, problems she didn't suspect intrude and demand constant adjustment of her girlhood dreams. A businessman, on the data available, decides on the future of the market for his product and conducts his business accordingly. But he knows full well that the completeness and accuracy of his information leave much to be desired. An artist creates a work of art, but he cannot be sure it will be considered as such.

Suppose an old beer can were produced, and someone offered to bet you that Charlie could not crush it. Would you take the bet? Now we have a situation full of risk and uncertainty—and a chance to make some money. Based on the information available, the bet seems like a fifty-fifty proposition. If you knew a little more about how strong Charlie was and the rigidity of the beer can, you could make a bet with the odds in your favor, provided the other fellow does not know what you know. But you could not be positive of the actual outcome.

And so it must be when we want something that everybody else wants, like money. At some point, chance must separate the winners from the losers. The more a person wants, the fiercer will be the competition and the greater the risks. What we hope to do in this book is to learn more than the other fellow and thereby acquire an advantage over him when playing the stock market.

Historically, our approach has justification. The study of games of chance has had enormous consequences for the physical sciences. I have always thought it odd that the same has not been true in the social sciences. After all, games of chance are as much concerned with people as with dice, or cards, or horses, or stocks.

It began in the middle of the seventeenth century, a time when gambling was immensely popular in the fashionable circles of French society. Huge amounts of money, personal honor, and possessions were staked on dice, cards, roulette, and many other games of chance. So much was involved that it was only natural that many people felt a need for a deeper understanding of what was going on. Such a person was the Chevalier de Méré, an ardent gambler and a close observer of the gambling scene. De Méré had a problem, now known as de Méré's paradox. He had figured out to his own satisfaction that the chances of rolling at least one ace in four throws of a die were the same as the chances of rolling at least one double ace in twenty-four throws of two dice. Yet, in actual games, he incurred steady losses on this bet, for, as he was quick to notice, the rolling of one ace in four throws of a single die, occurred slightly more than half the time, while the rolling of at least one double ace in twenty-four throws of two dice occurred slightly less than half the time. After having puzzled in vain over the difference between what he thought should happen and what actually did happen, de Méré turned for help to the great French scientist, mathematician, and philosopher, Blaise Pascal.

From what strange and unexpected directions the great advances come! Pascal took an immediate interest in the whole subject of gambling. In his studies and those of Fermat, Bernoulli, and d'Alembert, the mathematical theory of probability had its beginnings. Almost every mathematician of note furthered its development, and today, not only is it a major and active branch of mathematics in its own right, but it lies at the heart of all the physical sciences, the fundamental laws of which are probabilistic. It enters into more and more practical activities such as insurance, engineering, weather forecasting, economics, polling—anything requiring a prediction. One might say that a subject becomes scientific and meaningful only when it is firmly based on probability theory.

The use of probability implies that a given cause has multiple effects, or a given effect may have many causes. For example, when the weatherman tells us that there is a 50% chance of rain tomorrow, he means that present meteorological conditions have in the past led to rain on 50% of the following days. When a coin is flipped and you call heads, you have a fifty-fifty chance of being right—that is, you have a 50% chance of being right and a 50% chance of being wrong. In our routine life activities, fortunately, we stand much better than a fifty-fifty chance of doing the right thing. Life would be rather awkward if there were a fifty-fifty chance of losing our balance every time we took a step or of getting hit by a car every time we crossed the street. But we need not worry too much. A billion years of evolution have ensured that our bodies have a very high probability of doing what we want. If this were not the case, we would not be here today. As George Gaylord Simpson puts it, we are "evolution-tested." The whole process of the evolution of life forms may be looked

5

upon as nature's rather brutal way of forcing conformity to the realities of our earthly environment by changing the odds on survival to favor an adapting species. Our pre-human ancestors who lived in the sea did not sprout legs and develop lungs just because they felt like taking a walk on land. They changed form so as to be able to return to water when cast up on the shore by the sea or when the water in which they lived dried up. Our more recent ancestors were the failures when, with the disappearance of much of the forests, they were thrown out of their tree Garden of Eden by the ancestors of the great apes and had to make their way on the ground. The slaughter must have been terrific, and only those able to develop human qualities and abilities survived.

In our present technological society, matters usually go as we expect. We turn on a television set or start a car, and they work nearly all the time. What many scientists and engineers and businessmen created only after many years of tormenting, frustrating research and development is reduced to a simple, routine operation. But we can never be 100% certain of anything. After all, people do fall, and they do get hit by cars, and television sets and cars do not always work. Let's take a close look at what happens when a person crosses the street. Normally, he stops, looks, and listens. If his eyes and ears present no danger signals to his mind, he assumes the way is clear and crosses, successfully most of the time. But what about someone who does get hit? For one reason or another, danger has not registered: his picture of the street and the cars was not in accord with the realities of the situation. Like Charlie, he was not aware of all pertinent information.

We come to the fundamental problem that we shall face in this book and that each and every one of us must face during every moment of our existence. It has concerned philosophers at least since the time of Socrates, and it lies at the heart of all the great tragedies and comedies of the literary greats. *To what*

6

extent does reality correspond to what I think is reality? This is a very subtle problem indeed, one which people have learned to handle adequately only in this century. Notions of probability theory are involved, and probability is perhaps the most mature and sophisticated subject with which man has ever coped.

We usually accord to the expert in a field the most correct view of reality. If trouble develops in your television set or your car or yourself, you call in a service man or physician who can deal with this particular piece of reality more competently than you. On the other hand, a psychopath's view of reality is considered so dangerous that he is locked up. Here we have our first hint of what it takes to make money—we pay people when they know more about reality than we do.

Long before there was any deep understanding of natural environment, man knew a great deal about human nature. Inanimate nature was peopled with good and evil spirits who had human characteristics and all events were attributed to them. Spirits with human characteristics could be bargained with, cajoled, flattered, served, and dominated, and for this a great variety of rites was employed to assist people in attaining their desires. Sometimes these devices were successful and sometimes they were not. But I am sure those early people were quite aware of the complexity around them in the world and were wise enough not to expect 100% success from their picture of reality. That is more than I can say for many of today's so-called intellectuals, who do not seem to make any distinction between theory and reality. In the course of centuries, man's ideas of reality approximated more and more closely the actual state of affairs, and he was able to increase his control of his environment. This process has greatly accelerated in the last three hundred years with the rise of the scientific method.

Unfortunately, our understanding of human nature has not

7

progressed as much, probably because of the extreme complexity of all situations involving human relationships. Charlie's experience is a mild example of how unknown and uncontrollable forces can plague even the simplest attempts to study people, and should serve as a warning to people prone to discovering easy truths. What it all boils down to is that you cannot put people in a cage for study and experimentation, where the "slings and arrows of outrageous fortune" can be isolated and examined one by one. The consequent lack of experimental verification of almost all theories involving people—theories of history, government, economics, behavior—makes them suspect to any intelligent person. The enormous success of the scientific method has been due to the ability of scientists to set up experiments in which uncontrollable influences are minimized. Don't be fooled by all that fantastically complex apparatus that you see around a laboratory: scientists are really very simple people, and they deal only with relatively simple matters. They need all that apparatus mainly to isolate what they are studying from disturbing forces. Only in this way can they concentrate their attention upon one or two factors affecting the phenomena under study and be reasonably sure of learning something. Outside the laboratory, scientists become like everyone else, continually beset and befuddled by so many thousands of variables that they too wonder at times how the world carries on.

Where does that leave us? Basically, we wish to learn how to make money more proficiently, and we cannot do it in a laboratory. But fortunately games of chance furnish superb conditions for an investigation of the money-making process. The possible outcomes in each game are limited and well-defined. The realities of the world, as seen by the players, are completely summed up by the odds they are willing to accept. And finally, the full apparatus of the theory of probability is available for use. We shall pass from the very narrow world

8

of the simple games of chance to the almost all-inclusive world of the stock market. This great expansion of our horizons cannot be achieved without dealing in much more uncertainty, but actually, the very complexity of the stock market forces us to simplification, since most factors are too complicated to handle with any assurance.

One more point remains to be touched on in this chapter. Suppose we do have a system for picking stocks. We cannot expect all stocks picked by the system to go up in price. Some will go up, some down, and some will remain unchanged. How are we to judge the worth of the system?

CHAPTER II

FLIP-FLOP

For a deeper understanding of human nature, the game's the thing.

MARVIN B. SCOTT

YOUR broker calls you one day and suggests that Tough Gus, Inc., will probably go up and that you ought to buy it. If you are virginal in matters of securities, you take the advice without further ado. If you are a bit more sophisticated, you ask for the reasons behind the recommendation. You will then get all kinds of persuasion: it looks good on the chart, the fundamentals are good, and besides, our research department has investigated it thoroughly and they are experts. So you buy. If you are very sophisticated, you sell the stock short, figuring that by the time the people in Wall Street hear about something good, the stock is apt to be temporarily overpriced.

For most of us, our encounters with probability are largely intuitive. We buy a stock because we *assume* it will go up. We take a trip in an airplane because we *assume* the chances of an accident are small. We eat mushrooms because they are good and we *assume* that they were selected by an expert and are not poisonous. Our assumptions in these commonplace situations usually stand us in good stead. But very few of us are going to assume our way to a fortune, mainly because our assumptions and emotional reactions are hardly unique, and we share them in common with almost everyone else. A fortune is a rarity, and only a few exist. So it is essential that we render more precise our assumptions about reality.

Suppose we start by considering some problems in a simple game of chance, coin tossing. You and I agree to flip an unbiased coin for as long as I wish. Every time I call the toss correctly, you pay me a dollar, and every time I miss, I pay you a dollar. I am sure you would consider this a fair game since we both have a 50% chance of being right and the same chance of being wrong. After a number of tosses, it is quite likely that neither of us would be winning much money. But the phrase "quite likely" implies that there is a chance that this may not be so and that one of us could be a big winner. So, to reveal the deeper aspects of the problem, we ask the following question: If I start with ten dollars, all of which I am willing to risk in the game, what are my chances of increasing this amount to one thousand dollars before losing the ten dollars? Although such a problem belongs in the domain of the mathematical theory of probability,* we need concern ourselves only with the answer, which is quite simple. I have one chance in one hundred of increasing my capital from ten dollars to one thousand dollars before losing the ten dollars I started with. If I play the same game with each of many thousands of players, I will find that in one game in one hundred, I will increase my capital to one thousand dollars, thereby winning $990, but in ninety-nine games in one hundred, I will lose my starting ten dollars. So, overall, I am left with my initial ten dollars and have not made any money.

---

* For a lucid account of the theory, see, for example, *An Introduction to Probability Theory and its Applications,* by William Feller, published by John Wiley & Sons, New York. For those readers mathematically inclined, see Appendix A.

There is very little I can do about making money in this kind of game. No amount of intuition, extra-sensory perception, good luck charms, black magic, astrology, or mathematical knowledge will be of any help. In any one game I have a small, one-in-a-hundred chance of getting one thousand dollars. But there is no way of predicting when that game will occur. If it happens on the very first game I play and I stop playing, I will have been very lucky, like a person with a winning sweepstakes ticket. After many games, however, my luck is sure to run out. The point here is that there is no money to be made in a fair game, one in which both opponents have the same mathematical chance to win a given amount of money.

Now let's change the ground rules ever so slightly. Suppose I slip into the game a coin that, instead of coming up heads fifty times in every hundred flips, comes up heads fifty-one times, and suppose further that you are not aware of what I have done. Now, I always call heads, and you will be amazed to learn that my chances of turning ten dollars into one thousand dollars are one in three. If I play each of my opponents with that same coin, I will win $990 every third game and lose ten dollars two games in every three. My net profit will be $970 for every three games I play, a fantastic rate of gain on the thirty dollars risked in the three games. Knowing just a little more than my opponents about the realities of the situation gives me a tremendous advantage. Once again, there is nothing that can be done to change the odds in this game. If all my partners persist in playing me under these conditions, I am almost certain to win all the money they care to put up. To make the game fair, I should win only 96¢ when I make a right call and still pay you a dollar when I am wrong.

This last game is an example of a "favorable" game for me, since I am more apt to win than lose. But it must be emphasized that even in a favorable game, I am not certain to win.

12

There is always what gamblers call a probability of ruin. In our example, I expect to lose my initial capital of ten dollars in two games out of every three, so if ten dollars were all the money I had to my name, it is probable that I would be wiped out before I could make the thousand dollars. If, however, we agree to reduce the amount of each bet to 50¢ instead of a dollar, I could expect to get my one thousand dollars in forty-five games out of every hundred and lose my initial capital of ten dollars in only fifty-five games. My ruin probability is reduced. The greater my initial capital is than the amount staked on each bet, the less my chances of losing it. I would also be playing more safely if I were willing to accept less profit. If my ambition were merely to double my ten dollars, my chances of doing so before losing the ten dollars are six in ten. In the case where I have an infinite amount of money to put in the game, it is absolutely certain that you would lose everything you risked if you continued playing with me. The reason that on rare occasions someone breaks the bank at Monte Carlo is that the bank is only very rich, not infinitely rich.

In any game of chance, in life itself, three things must be considered when undertaking a course of action: (1) the probability of occurrence for all results that can be foreseen; (2) the benefit or profit to be derived if the action is successful; and (3) the probability of ruin. Juggling these points can be rather involved even in a relatively simple situation, like driving a car, for example. Suppose you decide to drive your car into town. You feel that the probability of arriving in town this way is excellent and that the benefit to you is worthwhile—the game is favorable. But there is a probability of ruin arising from two sources. First, you run the risk of losing your life by driving. Since 50,000 people out of 200,000,000 in this country are killed in automobile accidents every year, there is approximately one chance in 4000 of your losing your life. People who drive consider this possibility negligible. Second, there is a chance of killing somebody else in an accident and, as a result, losing all your money in a law suit. To circumvent this, most people play an unfavorable game by taking out liability insurance. Any insurance is unfavorable in that you are more likely to pay in to the insurance company more money than you will ever get out. If this were not true, the companies would go out of business. But the avoidance of ruin makes this unfavorable game one worth playing.

The only other reason to play unfavorable games is to give your money away either for enjoyment, or out of ignorance. In unfavorable games of this kind the lure of a big payoff frequently blinds the players to the near certainty of the loss of their risk money. Let's return to the coin tossing game to see how bad the chances are. Suppose now *you* know the coin is biased and will come up heads fifty-one times in every hundred flips. If you always call heads, what are my chances of doubling my starting $10 before losing it? It turns out that I have four chances in ten of ending up with $20 before losing $10. So if I play each of my adversaries on this basis, I will lose $10 in six games and win $10 in four games on average, which gives me a net loss of $20 for every ten games I play. Because I have risked $100 in the ten games, I have a 20% loss on my investment. If I want to end up with $1000 starting with $10, my chances are just about impossible. In only one game in 100,000,000,000,000,000 would I do so, while in 99,999,999,999,999,999 games I would lose $10 each. There is nothing anyone can do to turn an unfavorable game like this into a favorable one. All systems you may hear about are just gibberish. And, to make matters worse, most of the games we play in casinos or elsewhere are even more unfavorable than the one described.

But, fortunately or unfortunately, reality is far more complex than these simple exercises in probability theory. These

14

exercises are examples of the artificial school problems I mentioned earlier. In our examples, we used coins whose chances for coming up heads and tails were assumed known. Only then could we use the theory of probability to determine the behavior of the coins in a game of coin tossing. But in real life, in any game using a real coin, we never know for sure whether the coin is fair, or whether it is biased towards heads or tails. Suppose we check out a coin before using it in a game by flipping it one hundred times, and suppose it comes up heads forty-nine times and tails fifty-one times. Is this a biased coin?

The answer to this problem requires some rather sophisticated analysis into which we need not go too deeply. It is typical of the problems that scientists face constantly. Suffice it to say that the question is unanswerable with only one hundred flips. However, if the coin were flipped 1,000,000 times and it came up heads 480,000 times, the scientist would say with much confidence, but not absolute certainty, that the coin is biased. Now, nobody is going to flip a coin one million times. So the coin's true nature is unknown in any actual game. If you participate in a game of coin tossing, you will undoubtedly assume the coin is fair. Later events may lead you to revise your notion of reality, and if so, you will have become sadder and wiser for the experience.

Like all questions in life, there are no certain answers, even in this simple bit of experience. A reasonable person will naturally think of the coin as being fair or almost so. But an extremist on one side could just as well maintain that the coin has only a 10% chance of coming up heads in any one flip and that in one hundred flips there is a chance of getting forty-nine heads. This is so, although the probability is very, very small. The same would apply to an extremist on the other side who maintains the coin has a 90% chance of coming up heads. Where to draw the line between the reasonable and the unreasonable is a very difficult problem. For the coin under discussion, most scientists would say that the coin has a probability of coming up heads in the range of 40% to 60%. For a probability outside this range, there is less than a 1% chance of obtaining forty-nine heads in one hundred flips, and 1% is usually taken as the dividing line between a reasonable and unreasonable picture of reality.

In games of chance run by gambling establishments, it's you against the house. And rest assured, they have figuratively flipped the coin a million times. They know the true probabilities involved in their games well enough to set the return on a winning bet low, low enough to prevent anyone from developing a favorable system of play. If this were not so, there would be no gambling houses. In a game of roulette, for example, there are eighteen black numbers, eighteen red numbers, and two house numbers which are neither red nor black, a total of thirty-eight numbers. If you bet one dollar on a black number, you have, theoretically, eighteen chances of winning a dollar and twenty chances of losing a dollar. Although these chances are not exactly equal to the actual probabilities that exist for each wheel because of slight mechanical deviations, there is little doubt that they are close enough so that the house need not worry about favorable systems of play coming along. Your chances of turning $10 into $20 by making one dollar bets on black or red are only one in four. In every fourth game on average, you will win $10, but you will lose $30 in the other three games, which is a net loss of $20 on the $40 risked in the four games, a 50% loss of initial capital. Never forget that the house is in business to take your money away, and their view of the real probabilities is apt to be better than yours.

A person making a bet usually has little idea of the probabilities involved. He is concerned only with his hunches, good-luck charms, and superstitions, anything that will aid him in winning a single bet. The probabilities become apparent

16

only after many bets, by losses built up if the game is un-favorable and gains if the game is favorable. An insurance company knows with a high degree of accuracy how many people of age seventy will die in the next year, though for any one person, your guess is as good as anybody's. The probabilities are all that can be known. The person who knows them most accurately will be in closest touch with reality and will do best.

CHAPTER III

HORSE SENSE

> "By some intricate process, the thousands of diverse opinions of thousands of diverse people clash, interact, and modify one another in such a way that the final ensemble opinion is a closer approximation of the truth than that of any single individual."
>
> BURTON P. FABRICAND, *Horse Sense*

WE are off to the races. Not to bet, but to study the sociology of a game that is remarkably similar to the stock market. Because it is not as complex as the market, we shall be able to treat the game of horse betting rather thoroughly and arrive at some new and fundamental ideas which will turn out to be extremely fruitful. Up till now, the probabilities in the games we have considered, coin tossing and roulette, are mechanically fixed and generally known to a high degree of approximation. If you gamble in a casino, you are willing to pay for the privilege by accepting a return that is less than necessary to break even over many bets. It's you against the house, and the odds are strongly in favor of the house. You may win once in a while, but if you continue playing, the house is almost certain to take all your money.

At the races, the situation is different. A person wishing to bet on a horse puts up a stake with the race track, in return for which he receives a ticket giving the details of the transaction, the horse, the amount bet, the date, and so on. The track collects all the money bet in a pool and deducts a certain percentage, usually around 15%, as a commission for itself and the state. When the race is over, the track hands out the remaining money to those holding tickets on the winning horse. The track acts merely as a broker. What makes this game different from casino games is that the return on a winning bet is determined not by the track, but by the collective opinion of all the bettors on the horse's chances of winning at the start of the race. It's not you against the track, but you against all the other bettors, your opinion against theirs. The game of horse betting is as much concerned with people as with horses.

You may have the idea that horse racing is a completely unpredictable game. After all, such queer things can and do happen at the track. A horse, holding a substantial lead in the stretch and apparently a certain winner, decided that swimming was preferable to running. Whereupon he unseated the jockey, hurdled the restraining hedge, and dove into the infield lake, drowning before he could be rescued. Another, a heavily bet favorite, was pulled up a mile before the finish by his rider, the best jockey of the time, because of a miscount in the number of times he was supposed to circle the track. At the starting bell, another horse backed out the gate and took off in the opposite direction. But all these strange events just show that the same lack of certainty exists at the races as everywhere else. A little further study will show us that great regularity exists when the probabilities are considered, as in the simpler games of the last chapter.

The probabilities of interest to us are those for the winning chances of each of the horses in a race. Now, nobody knows for certain each horse's probability of winning, so each bettor must estimate for himself the probability of winning and whether or not the return he gets if the horse wins is worth the risk of betting. If he decides a horse has a 50% chance of winning, he must win a dollar for each dollar bet if the horse wins, just to break even over many bets of this sort. For if he is correct in his probability assignments, half the horses which he thinks have a fifty-fifty chance of winning will win.

How a bettor fares depends on how realistic his probability estimates are. If they are more correct than those of his opponent, he will do better. If they are not as good, he will do worse. Unfortunately for horse bettors, they are up against a very formidable opponent, the betting public, whose estimates of the true winning probabilities can only be described as superb. Through some fantastically intricate process, the thousands of diverse opinions of thousands of diverse people clash, interact, and modify one another in such a way that the final ensemble opinion is a closer approximation of the truth than that of any single individual. Since this is the case, the payoff on a winning bet is usually so low as to make the game extremely unfavorable. Much more unfavorable, in fact, than the coin tossing and roulette examples discussed earlier.

For those interested, the mathematical details of the way this state of affairs comes about are given in Appendix B. Here, I will describe in words what happens at the track.

Each bettor at the track decides on the horse he thinks most likely to succeed and backs his opinion by betting his money. The money from all bettors is collected in a pool. Now suppose that 10% of all the money in the pool is bet on Buzz Fuzz. What the public is saying is this: based on all the information available at the start of the race, Buzz Fuzz has a 10% chance of winning the race. More generally, any horse in any race with 10% of all the money in the pool bet on it has a 10% chance of winning the race, according to the public. Or, putting it another way, one-tenth of those horses with 10% of the public's money riding on them should win if the public is correct in its probability estimates.

If the public has estimated the probabilities accurately and a person bets one dollar on each of ten horses of this type, he can expect to have one winner and nine losers. To break even, he must win $9 on his one winner to make up for nine losers. But, unfortunately, he will win only $7.50 on his one winner, and, therefore, over ten bets he will lose $1.50, or 15% of the total amount of $10 bet. This 15% loss is the commission extracted by the track.

Similarly, if 50% of the money in the win pool is bet on a horse, the public thinks this horse has a 50% chance of winning. But the profit on this horse if it wins is only 70¢ for each dollar bet. If the public is correct in its thinking about the race, a bettor must win on half of these horses. So, for each race he wins 70¢, there will be a race on which he loses a dollar, giving him a net loss of 30¢ for every two dollars bet, again a 15% loss on the amount bet.

Everything hinges on how good the public's thinking is about the chances of all horses in all races. It turns out, as demonstrated in Appendix B, that the public's probability estimates are remarkably close to the actual probabilities that exist at the races. By this I mean that horses to which the public assigns a 10% probability of winning actually do win very nearly 10% of the time, horses to which the public assigns a 50% probability of winning actually do win nearly half of the time. And if this is the case, a bettor will lose 15% of the amount he bets and there is very little that he can do about it. He may win a race or have a lucky streak now and then, but over the long run he will almost certainly lose all the money he cares to risk in this very unfavorable game.

Another remarkable result concerns the favorite in a race, the horse on which the most money is bet. The favorite is the best bet in a race. A person betting only on favorites will fare

21

better than any other wagerer, and better than if he played the selections of any of the expert handicappers. This situation arises because the public's probability estimates for favorites are slightly on the low side. Not only does the public determine winning probabilities very accurately for all horses, but it determines them in such a way that the public choices do best. Many excuses are offered for the relatively poor showing of the experts. But whatever the excuses, the discrepancy between the performances of their selections and the public's choices is so consistently great that there can be only one valid reason—the betting public is more expert.

There is a question of how and by whom the favorite is determined. Is it by some small group of people who know more than anybody else or is it by the public as a whole? If the former is the case, it would be a very bankrupt group whose capital is continually drained away by the unfavorable game they are playing. All indications point to the likelihood of the latter estimate. In the first place, half the total volume of wagering on each race is accounted for by the $2 and $5 bets, and it would be unbelievable if the distribution of these bets among all the horses differed appreciably from bets of higher value, most of which are $10 bets. And secondly, a simple count of the number of people lining up before the $2 payoff windows reveals far greater numbers lined up when a favorite wins than compared to any other choice. There is little doubt that the choosing of a favorite is a phenomenon involving full public participation.

To be sure, anyone betting on the favorite in every race in a large enough sample of races will lose money, but he will lose only about 9% of what he bets, which is less than anyone not betting favorites, and less than the 15% commission. But suppose the commission were only 1%. What a marvelous way to make money horse betting would be! Just betting the public favorite in every race you would win on average 5%

of what you bet. If you bet $100 on each of the nine races that make up the daily card, your winnings would average 5% of $900 or $45 daily. Considering the existing 15% take (and these commissions seem to be going up steadily), however, your only chance of making money is to find those races, if they exist, wherein the public errs in its assessment of the winning probabilities. But why bother, when there is a different game available where the commission is only about 1% and money-making opportunities abound. I am speaking of the stock market, which will occupy our attention for the remainder of this book.

CHAPTER IV

A FAVORABLE GAME IS THE STOCK MARKET

"Speculation ... is the self-adjustment of society to the probable. Its value is well-known as a means of avoiding or mitigating catastrophes, equalizing prices and providing for periods of want. It is true that the success of the strong induces imitation by the weak, and that incompetent persons bring themselves to ruin by undertaking to speculate in their turn. But legislatures and courts generally have recognized that the natural evolutions of a complex society are to be touched only with a very cautious hand...."

OLIVER WENDELL HOLMES

OCTOBER, according to Mark Twain, is one of the peculiarly dangerous months to speculate in. The others are July, January, September, April, November, May, March, June, December, August, and February. Many people take this advice and stuff their money in an old shoe, or in savings accounts, or in safe bonds. However, unfortunately for these people, the inexorable rise in the cost of living over the years has cost them dearly. The protection of one's capital requires its investment in a game sufficiently favorable to overcome inflationary living costs. Consider the twenty-five-year period from 1940 to 1965 as an example. A person keeping his money in a savings account drawing the average 4% interest during this time would have seen his principal grow to almost three times the original amount. Large as this may seem, it was not enough to keep pace with the cost of living. Stocks, on the other hand, not only yielded more than 4% in dividends but increased about seven times in value during this period!

Is the stock market the favorable game we are looking for?

Long ago man recognized the utility of investing money. As civilization advanced, he learned to produce in excess of his immediate needs and accumulate the surplus for later consumption by himself and others. Money itself became a means for the storage of goods and services for future use in addition to its use as a medium of exchange between hunter, artisan, and farmer.

When the need arose for the transportation of goods to distant places in ships costing sums of money greatly in excess of the amounts possessed by single individuals, it was but a step to the notion of multiple ownership of vessels and cargoes. Groups of merchants stocked ships for foreign trade and depended on astute captains to exchange domestic surpluses for foreign goods or gold on a favorable basis. From such joint ventures evolved the publicly owned corporation of today, which is an extremely effective device for channeling many small bits of capital towards one common goal. When corporations are managed properly, the financial rewards to the many owners of the corporation are exceeded only by the immense benefits to the public, which gains from the cheaper production and more widespread distribution of goods and services. Not to be lost sight of, however, is the fact that the whole process is made possible by the individual investors, who act in hope of receiving future income benefits from hoarded present day savings.

Much as the odds in horse betting, the return on an investment in a stock is governed by what investors collectively think of the company. A person buying the stock of some company thinks that his return on the money he puts up for the stock, either from price appreciation, dividends, or a combination of the two, minus the broker's commission of about 1%, may be greater than the return available elsewhere. A person selling a stock thinks he can do better either in another stock or in some other form of investment. In the market place for stocks, the opinions of these two groups of people continually clash, interact, and modify one another until a price level for a stock is reached at which there are about as many people thinking one way as the other. What the people as a whole, the investing public, are doing, then, is trying to decide a price for a stock that adequately reflects the risks involved in securing a good return on the investment. Each passing moment, the risks are evaluated and reevaluated by someone in the light of any new information that arises, and the market price of each stock will fluctuate with each revelation. The thoughts of millions of people concerning the prospects of the many businesses upon which our society relies are mirrored in the market quotations on the financial pages of the daily newspapers. What fantastic complexity, what unfathomable, unmeasurable forces underly each of these numbers!

How good is the public's estimate of the realities of the world as reflected in its determination of stock prices? Will stocks yield a return on invested capital at least as good as that obtainable elsewhere? How good are the predictions and advice of the experts? What are the chances of getting a return on investment greater than the expectations of the public? Is there a system for doing so? These are the important questions we will now consider.

Pick any stock and look at its price. The odds are overwhelming that its present price is higher than its price over most of its previous history. For example, the Dow-Jones average as this is being written is around 900, a figure which is higher than ever before except for a brief period in the beginning of 1966. This record indicates that the stock market goes up as time passes in spite of occasional breaks. If you risked a certain amount of money buying some stock at some time in the past, the chances are excellent that it is worth more now. Contrast this performance with what would have occurred were the money invested in one of the unfavorable games discussed in the previous chapters. There we learned that the loss of initial capital becomes a certainty if we continue playing. Here we have our first indication that the stock market is a favorable game, that we are more apt to win than lose when buying a stock.

How much?

It may be hard to believe, but despite immense quantities of available data, comparatively little in the way of definitive research has been done on the rates of return from investments in common stocks. Edgar Lawrence Smith, in a 1924 publication "Common Stocks as Longterm Investments," demonstrated that representative common stock lists had consistently outperformed standard bond investments over any ten-year period since the Civil War, taking into account both income return and price changes. N. Molodovsky, in a paper "Stock Values and Stock Prices" (from *Financial Analysts Journal,* May-June 1960, p. 81), showed that from 1871-1959, industrial common stocks yielded an average dividend of more than 5% and also increased in price at a compounded annual rate of 2.5%. Although these studies offer further confirmation of the favorable game nature of the stock market, they are far from the ideal way to measure expected returns.

The best way to measure rates of return on common stocks is as follows: pick a stock at random. Pick a purchase date at random and note the price. Pick a later sale date at random. Convert the difference in prices on the two dates into the percent return per annum compounded annually * needed to bring one's invested capital from the initial amount to the final amount, deducting buying and selling commissions and taking into account any dividends paid, whether cash or stock. Repeat the same process over and over again. Display the results in such a way that the number of completed transactions for each percent return per annum is easily seen.

Of course such a procedure for all stocks, listed and unlisted, for all time periods over stock market history would be hopelessly involved. In recent years, two important approximations to the above ideal have been carried out, and I now describe them.

Professors L. Fisher and J. H. Lorie, writing in *The Journal of Business of the University of Chicago,* Vol. XXXVII, No. 1, January 1964, measured rates of return on investments in common stocks listed on the New York Stock Exchange for twenty-two time periods from January 1926 to December 1960. They invested an equal sum of money in each company having one or more issues of listed common stock at the beginning of each period, noted its value at the end of the period, and calculated the percent return per annum compounded annually. The results are shown in Table I. Dividends were handled in three ways: (1) Dividends reinvested—any dividends in a period were reinvested as received in the stock of the same company; (2) Dividends not reinvested; (3) Dividends ignored. The "Dividends Reinvested" column shows the rates of return for the twenty-two periods, including dividends and capital appreciation. The "Dividends Ignored" column shows only the rate of capital appreciation without considera-

---

* Those readers not trusting their mathematical abilities may think of the percent return per annum compounded annually as the amount of interest a bank would have to pay on a savings account to bring the account from some initial amount of money to some final amount of money in the time allotted. In Appendix C the compound interest formula which summarizes this procedure is explained.

28

tion of dividends. The commissions paid for purchasing the stock are taken into account.

So consistently high are the rates of return that many readers must be rather surprised, especially those of conservative nature who have chosen investments with substantially lower average rates of return. Savings in commercial banks, mutual savings banks, and savings and loan associations never earned as much as 6% per annum for any of the twenty-two time periods and for most of the period 1926-1960 earned less than 4%. Municipal and United States government bonds, as indicated by Standard & Poor indices, averaged less than 4% during the twenty-two time periods. Corporate bond yields ranged from a minus 6% to just over 15% for the period 1900-1958, with the very high yields achieved during the recovery from the depression when prices of industrial bonds rose sharply. For most periods, yields varied between 5% and 8%. Yields realized on mortgage loans on non-farm homes from 1920-1947 never exceeded 6% and averaged about 5%.

Compare these returns with those in Table I. For the entire thirty-five year period 1926-1960, the rate of return compounded annually on common stocks listed on the New York Stock Exchange, with reinvestment of dividends, was 9%. Such a return will double your money in just eight years. For twelve of the twenty-two periods, the rates of return are above 11% per annum. For stocks bought at the beginning of the ten postwar periods covered, the return averaged 11%.

The worst losses occurred for investments made in September 1929, just before the great market crash of that year, and sold at the bottom of the Depression in 1932. Almost a 50% loss of capital was taken by the average investor for stocks owned outright. Those on margin lost correspondingly more. Such catastrophic losses, while unlikely, are always possible even in a favorable game. Many "safe" savings accounts also disappeared over this period.

29

TABLE I. Rates of return on investment in common stocks listed on the New York Stock Exchange in percent per annum compounded annually.

Period	Dividends Reinvested	Dividends Not Reinvested	Dividends Ignored
1/26-12/60	9.0%	6.9%	3.9%
-9/29	20.4	19.8	15.7
-6/32	−16.5	−13.2	−21.0
-12/40	2.4	1.6	−2.8
-12/50	6.8	5.1	1.3
9/29-6/32	−48.4	−48.2	−51.5
-12/40	−3.0	−4.9	−8.0
-12/50	4.9	2.3	−0.5
-12/60	7.7	4.9	2.5
6/32-12/40	21.3	24.5	16.9
-12/50	18.6	21.4	13.1
-12/60	17.4	20.5	11.9
12/50-12/52	12.5	12.6	5.9
-12/54	17.9	17.3	11.4
-12/56	17.0	16.6	10.8
-12/58	16.5	16.2	10.7
-12/60	14.8	15.0	9.6
12/55-12/56	6.4	6.5	1.5
-12/57	−3.7	−3.3	−8.3
-12/58	13.0	12.6	8.0
-12/59	14.0	13.7	9.3
-12/60	11.2	11.1	6.7

If you had selected a portfolio back in January 1926 by throwing darts at the financial page of a newspaper, you would most likely have attained in 1960 the same return on your money as Fisher and Lorie did, 9% per annum compounded annually. Every dollar invested in 1926 would have been worth over twenty dollars in 1960. Putting an equal amount of money into each stock, as did Fisher and Lorie, gives the same rate of return that would be available to an investor who picked stocks at random without exercising any judgment. If

30

only one or two stocks were picked by the dart method in 1926, almost any rate of return might have occurred, from a total loss to a gain of hundreds of percent. But, as the number of stocks selected is increased, the average return would close in on 9%. Again, we have a situation like that of the life insurance company, which knows very accurately how many people of a given age will die in the next year but cannot tell what person in any one case.

The evidence for the favorable game concept of the stock market mounts. In fact, it begins to appear that you cannot afford to stay out of the market. This idea was further developed in a later study by Professor Fisher. Recognizing the need for more time intervals, he published a much more extensive compilation of rates of return in *The Journal of Business of the University of Chicago,* Vol. XXXVIII, No. 2, April 1965. His results are based on the following random process: (1) Pick a stock at random from the 1715 common stocks that were listed on the New York Stock Exchange during the period January 1926 through November 1960; (2) Pick a purchase date at random from the final business day of the months during the period; (3) Pick a sale date at random later than the purchase date from the final business day of the months during the period from February 1926 through December 1960 if the stock is still listed; (4) Convert the difference in prices to a rate of return per annum compounded annually taking into account dividends and commissions. When a stock pays a dividend, the money is used to purchase additional shares of the stock at the end of the month.

Under this procedure, a stock can be held for periods varying from one month to thirty-five years. General Motors, for example, would show one-month holding periods beginning with the purchase of the stock on the final business day of January 1926 and the selling of the stock on the final business

31

day of February 1926. The final one-month holding period would begin with the purchase of the stock on the final business day of November 1960 and end with the sale of the stock on the final business day of December 1960. There would be two-month, three-month, . . . , thirty-four years and ten-month, thirty-four years and eleven-month, and thirty-five-year intervals. All would begin on the final business day of some month and end on the final business day of some later month. A stock like General Motors which was listed over the full thirty-five-year period would have twelve times thirty-five or 420 monthly holding periods, six times thirty-five or 210 two-month holding periods, . . . , and so on—ending in one thirty-five-year holding period.

The results are shown in Figure 1, which is derived from Fisher's paper. For some 1715 stocks, 56,557,538 holding periods, varying from one month to the full thirty-five-year period, went into this graph. The largest number of intervals yielded a return of about 10% per year compounded annually, as evidenced from the pronounced peak in the graph at this return. As we go away from the peak on either side, the number of intervals decreases smoothly towards zero. For 78% of these holding intervals, a profit was shown. These profitable intervals are represented by the white area under the curve. In 22%, a loss occurred, as shown by the dotted section of the graph. Over two-thirds of all the intervals yielded a rate of return in excess of 5%, a rate of return larger than that obtainable from savings accounts during that time. Nearly one-fifth of them had a return in excess of 20% per annum compounded annually, a rate which will double your money in under four years. One-half of the periods had rates of return greater than 9.8%, which, therefore, is the median return and is indicated on the graph. In 12,292,301 holding periods, a loss was incurred, and the investment was wiped out in 3045 periods. However, it appears that over the forty-year interval,

32

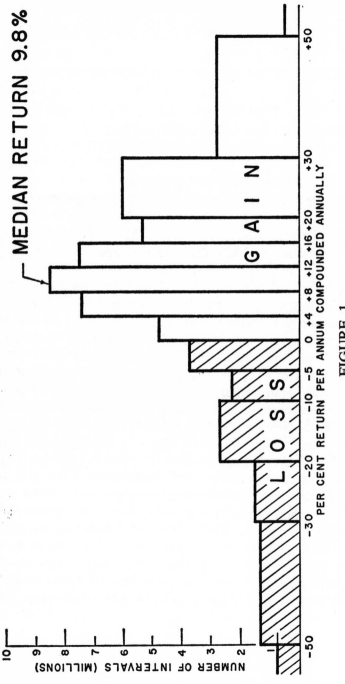

FIGURE 1

the probability of gain exceeded the probability of loss by a wide margin.

I mentioned above that the studies of Lorie and Fisher are not the ideal way to measures rates of return in the stock market, but only approximations. As such, they are open to criticism on the basis of the limited number of stocks and the relatively short time period considered. Still, when judged with the other evidence brought out in this chapter, the conclusion becomes inescapable that random selection of common stocks is a highly effective way of making money.

People talk about bull markets and bear markets as if all profits and losses averaged out to zero in the long run. If anything, the great declines, especially the one in 1929, are remembered more vividly than the rises and almost everyone is continually on the lookout for the next crash. But the weight of evidence points strongly in the other direction. The crashes are but temporary interruptions in a strong upward trend, a trend so strong that it would seem foolhardy for anyone not to invest at least part of his savings in the stock market. Of course, there will be times when money will be lost. We live in a world of uncertainties, and nobody can be sure of his savings no matter where he puts them. The number of mortgage foreclosures, the substantial rate of default on bonds, and the eradication of savings accounts during the 1930s show that even "conservative" investments carry considerable risk.

Horse racing is but a small slice of human experience, not nearly as complicated as other social phenomena. Yet, its complexity is such as to defy precise analysis by any individual, no matter how clever. How amazing and wonderful it is, then, that a large group of people, acting collectively, can determine with uncanny accuracy the underlying probabilities involved! Now, we have further evidence of the public's ability in the much more complex game of stocks. While it is not as rigorously valid as the evidence from horse racing, the extrapolation

34

from horses to stocks is made reasonable and convincing by the pari-mutuel aspect of both.

Therefore, I assert with confidence that the investing public determines the price of a stock at any time so that the rate of return from appreciation plus dividends is greater than that available from bonds and savings accounts. Some may say that future expectations are not guaranteed by past performance, but I see no reason to believe the public will not judge the future as well as it has in the past. After all, our evidence covers a period when two great world wars occurred, as well as an unprecedented breakdown in the economy of calamitous proportions. The rightness of the public is the basic reason why so many people have made money in the stock market.

CHAPTER V

THE WIGGLEWATCHERS

Every dog has its day.

ITEM in *The New York Times,* August 16, 1967: "A member of the Senate Banking Committee sought to prove today that it is possible to pick a portfolio of stocks that would do better than most mutual funds simply by throwing darts at the New York Stock Exchange list. Senator Thomas J. McIntyre, Democrat of New Hampshire, reported to the committee that he had done just that, and gotten better investment results than the average of even the most growth-oriented mutual funds. A hypothetical $10,000 investment made 10 years ago in the Senator's dart-selected stocks would be worth $25,300 now."

Senator McIntyre's dart-selected portfolio was as follows: Boston Edison, Cincinnati Milling Machinery, Crown Zellerbach, Colgate-Palmolive, Distillers Corporation-Seagrams Limited, Hammermill Paper, Harsco Corporation, Industria Electrica de Mexico, Minnesota Mining and Manufacturing, and Public Service Gas and Electric. Hardly a list with which to combat the selections of a growth-oriented fund. The results, however, which did not include reinvestment of dividends, were a bit better than those achieved over the 1957-1966 period by thirty-five growth category mutual funds.

Senator McIntyre was raising a question about the charges that mutual funds impose for managing their investors' money. He tried his experiment, he told the committee, after fund managers had disputed testimony given earlier by two noted economists that a random selection of stocks would yield investment results as good as or better than those achieved by the funds. The two economists were Henry C. Wallich of Yale University and Paul A. Samuelson of the Massachusetts Institute of Technology.

The *New York Times* article concluded with the observation that spokesmen for individual mutual funds made no serious attempt to answer the Senator though several jokingly offered him a job.

But is it a joke? Is chance more expert than the "experts"? Is the public more expert than the "experts"? Let us examine the record of the experts more closely, starting with the records of mutual fund performance.

A mutual fund is an organization that collects money from people and invests it for the purpose of capital growth from appreciation or dividends, or both. The fund managers spend full time investigating and analyzing investment opportunities and so, presumably, should be able to invest the fund's money in those stocks likely to do best. For their efforts, they receive a management fee.

1927-1935. "It can, then, be concluded with considerable assurance that the entire group of management investment companies proper (as opposed to the sample here studied) failed to perform better than an index of leading common stocks and probably performed somewhat worse than the index over the 1927-1935 period . . ." This statement is from "The Statistical Survey of Investment Trusts and Investment Companies," based on a compilation by the Securities and

Exchange Commission staff, as quoted in *Security Analysis* by Graham, Dodd, and Cottle, 1964, page 740. The results following are derived from the same book.

1934-1939. The overall gain in asset value of the six largest companies—Atlas Corporation, Dividend Shares, Incorporated Investors, Lehman Corporation, Massachusetts Investment Trust, and State Street Investment—averaged out to 53.7% including dividends paid out. Standard & Poor's 420 Stocks showed a 66.6% increase and only one of the funds exceeded this figure by achieving 70.6%.

1940-1949. In this period, the same six companies had an average gain of 129% in asset value including dividends, compared to 97% for Standard & Poor's 420 Stocks.

1951-1960. The performance of fifty-eight companies over this ten-year period, assuming that all distributions are reinvested in the companies' shares at the end of the year in which made, averaged to a gain of 221%, more than tripling the initial capital. But Standard & Poor's Composite Index of 500 common stocks showed a gain of 322%, almost 50% better than the average of the funds. This figure was exceeded by only three of the fifty-eight companies.

I quote Graham, Dodd, and Cottle: "These results do not appear to us to be as satisfactory as they should be. They suggest that the investment companies as a whole—and practicing security analysts as a whole—might well reexamine their basic approaches to both the selection of common stocks for purchase and the decision to sell 'less satisfactory' holdings."

1958-1967. In Figure 2, we see the performance of 146 funds over the ten-year period December 31, 1957 to December 31, 1967. The percent return per annum compounded annually needed to arrive at a fund's asset value as of December 31, 1967 starting from its asset value as of December 31, 1957 and including dividends and distributions is shown along the horizontal axis of the graph. Each bar represents those

38

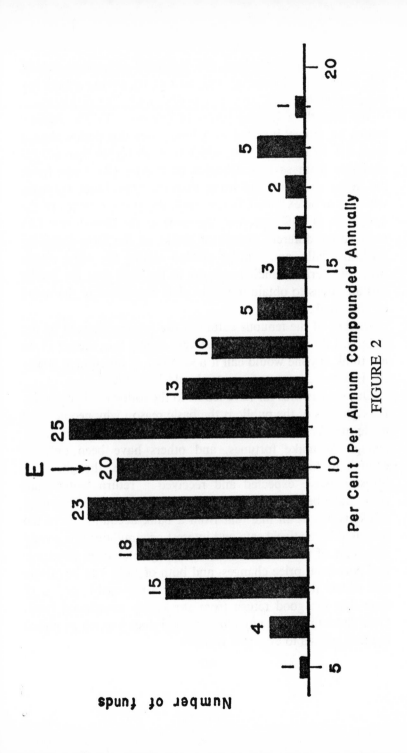

FIGURE 2

funds which have attained this indicated percentage return. The Dow-Jones industrial, rail, and utility averages each appreciated about 10% over this period, including dividends.

We note the following points of interest: (1) The percent return on money invested with funds over this period ranged from 5% to 19% per year, which is much higher than returns available from savings accounts or bonds; (2) some funds did better and some did worse than the Dow-Jones averages, which is to be expected, but, overall, the average return of the 146 funds is 10% per year, the same as the Dow-Jones; (3) such vastly different groups of stocks as the Dow-Jones industrials, rails, and utilities yielded almost the same return over this period, lending support to the idea that the public sets all prices to obtain a certain yield regardless of the name of the stock.

In view of the tenuous nature of the results obtained by the experts, I do not intend to delve very deeply into the art (I do not think anyone would call it a science) of investment analysis. However, some comments should be made.

Our studies thus far have led us to the following hypothesis: the rightness of the public is the basic reason why people have made money in the stock market. Some have been lucky enough to make fortunes, and others have been unlucky enough to lose all their money. On average, though, most investors have expected and received a return better than could have been obtained elsewhere. Of course, the return on stocks is not at all like that from a bank account, where the principal is relatively safe and interest accumulates at a steady rate. Part of the return from stocks originates from dividends and part from price changes, and both of these can be erratic and widely fluctuating. It is only over a reasonable period of time that the good return from stocks has manifested itself. Over short intervals, anything can and does happen as public opinion adjusts to ever new realities.

From this point of view, the fundamental assumption of stock market analysts is brought into focus. Stock analysts think they are better judges of the uncertainties existing in the world than the public as a whole. Broadly speaking, they form two groups, one using a "fundamental" approach and the other a "technical" approach. The fundamentalist considers all the voluminous statistics available both on the economy and on individual corporations, and tries to decide whether or not a stock is fairly priced in relation to this data. Later, we shall see in detail how he does this. In general, he must project his view of the national and international political and monetary scene, proceed from there to measure the smooth evolution of demand and supply factors in the various sectors of the economy, determine the rate of earnings growth for the company under examination in the light of all these factors, and finally come up with a price for the stock that adequately discounts the future growth of earnings. Quite an undertaking!

The technical approach shuns all such data and tries to forecast stock market behavior mainly by the analysis of price movements. This technical theory had its origin more than sixty years ago when Charles H. Dow, then editor of *The Wall Street Journal*, noted that the price movements of the stock market averages resembled the pattern of ocean tides. One can easily tell when the tide is as high and as low as it will get, and Dow pursued the analogy to stock prices in a series of articles, the substance of which has become known as the Dow Theory. Briefly, the Dow Theory postulates that a trend in being may be expected to persist on its course, like the tide, until it gives evidence of reversing itself. At a reversal point, a "bull market" or a "bear market" signal is said to be given. However, the extent to which the ocean tides and the Dow Theory correspond to the changes in the prices of stocks has never been demonstrated with finality. From the evidence presented thus far, any similarity is purely coincidental, and occurs only in the mind of the beholder.

Analysis of the price pattern alone is not the sole concern of the technician. Other factors are considered, such as insider buying and selling, what the mutual funds are doing, the short interest, price trends as defined in any one of many ways, and the relative price action of a stock as compared to the action of other stocks.

Implicit in the technical approach is the idea that the numbers which represent stock prices contain all the information necessary to predict the future. Based on this approach, one could suggest that stock prices are endowed with a memory that affects all subsequent behavior. Actually, most technicians do not go this far. They do believe, however, that their methods can uncover favorable corporate developments before the information becomes too widespread and before the price of the stock has risen out of sight.

I term both the fundamentalists and the technicians "wigglewatchers," since they are forever trying to correlate wiggles on their graphs with the wiggles in stock prices. But, unfortunately, the correlating techniques are usually handled very crudely, and each person sees just about what he wants in all those variegated wiggles. To my knowledge, all valid statistical studies of correlations have cast great doubt on the simple cause and effect nature of these factors. If any system based purely on wiggles were to succeed, everyone would find out about it and everyone would get rich.

I might cite the late Edmund W. Tabell, who was considered the dean of chartists until he died in 1965. Tabell never claimed infallibility. In fact, he said he was right only about 70% of the time. Now being right 70% of the time sounds very nice. But let us not forget the studies of Fisher and Lorie covered in the last chapter. There we saw that on the basis of random investment a gain resulted 78% of the time. It would seem that the technician with all his elaborate charting methods can do no better than dart throwers.

I might include among the experts the modern electronic computer, since many people seem to think that this complex apparatus will be able to find a valid system for picking stocks. There are two things to keep in mind always when dealing with computers. One is GIGO—garbage in, garbage out. The other is that a computer is dumber than anybody. It is ridiculous to think that a computer is going to come up with an idea when the user cannot.

Some further examples of expert performance may be enlightening. I quote from *Missiles and Rockets,* September 14, 1964: "Communication Satellite Corp. stock, which has more than doubled in price since its initial offering to the public in June, continues its upward movement. But some professionals say it's happening for the wrong reasons.

"It is now viewed in some quarters as a very sound long-term investment judged on its own merits. The major reason its price has moved so rapidly to high ground, however, is basically an amazing scarcity of shares for daily trading—in combination with some rather short-sighted short-selling of the issue based in large measure on early, perhaps overly pessimistic, views of its likely performance.

" 'The instinct of the public, in this case,' says George P. Edgar of the security consulting firm of the same name, 'has operated better than that of Wall Street. For the most part, professionals have missed ComSat and the public took the ball and ran.' " Edgar goes on to show that at least 80% of the outstanding five million public shares are represented by the odd-lot buyers. Wall Street professionals failed to understand the attractive fundamentals of ComSat, and many were even prompted to sell the stock short. At least one over-the-counter firm ceased operating as a result of a large loss in handling ComSat.

We come now to a very interesting and very subtle problem. If someone claims that he has a good way to predict stock prices, how can we prove him right or wrong? How can we test his claim? Certainly we do not expect him to be right all the time, yet how much of the time should he be right to be believed?

The evaluation of any system or theory requires that it be stated in such terms that it is possible to recognize when results come from blind chance. In too many instances, tests for the validity of theories are either neglected, overlooked, or impossible to make. In consequence, too many ridiculous statements are bruited about by supposedly intelligent men and women. Take the following anecdote, for example, which caricatures well what passes for research in many areas.

A medical research man, testing the effects of a new drug on cancer in chickens, was overjoyed to find that it seemed to cure in a high percentage of cases. Word of his success quickly spread, and he was invited to address a medical convention. In his talk, he described the drug, his techniques, and finally his results. These he reported as follows: "An amazingly high percentage of the chickens, one-third of them, showed great improvement. In one-third of them, there seemed to be no effect, and, er—the other chicken ran away."

Fortunately for our purposes, the proper way to determine the validity of a stock selection system is rather simple. The method comes from a branch of mathematics known as combinatorial analysis and goes under the name of *ballot problems*. To illustrate, suppose someone claims to be able to predict the price action of stocks. We say fine, and tell him to give us a list of fifteen stocks that he likes and fifteen stocks that he does not like. At the end of six months or any other agreeable time period, we will be able to compare the percentage changes in prices.

Before going on, let me make an aside for those who are not

44

sure that they understand what a percentage change is. In the fall of 1967, I owned a stock called Welbilt Corporation, one of the cheapest stocks listed on the New York Stock Exchange. Soon after I had bought it, it became very active and went from $4 to $6 a share in two or three days. Nothing at all was mentioned in the newspaper columns about this huge 50% gain in price. At about the same time, International Business Machines stock gained fifteen points in a single day, and the columns were full of stories about IBM skyrocketing in price. But IBM was selling at about $600 a share at the time, and for it to have made a gain comparable to that of Welbilt, it would have had to go up three hundred points. An investor putting $10,000 into Welbilt at $4 a share would have shown a profit of $5000, but a $10,000 investment in IBM would have shown a profit of only $250.

The number of points a stock goes up or down compared to its original price is the important thing; this is the percentage change in price. Welbilt stock went up two points from $4 a share to $6 a share. If we divide the change in price, 2, by the original price, 4, we get one-half or 50% for the percentage change in price. IBM gained fifteen points from a price of $600 a share to a price of $615 a share, and if we divide 15 by 600, we get .025 or 2.5% for the percentage gain. So a person putting $10,000 into Welbilt would have shown a gain of 50% on his money or $5000, while a person putting $10,000 into IBM would have shown a gain of 2.5% on his money. If a stock goes down, there is a percentage loss on the investment, which is calculated by dividing, as before, the change in price by the original price.

As far as specific stock predictions are concerned, we will consider those made by a respected investment service, The Value Line Investment Survey. The Value Line groups stocks into five groups, or categories, and suggests that Group I stocks should outperform Group II stocks, Group II stocks

GROUP I

Stock	Price 8/3/67	2/1/68	% Change
American Bakeries	27	24	−11%
Am. Crystal Sugar	23	27	17
Am. Machine & Foundry	24	22	−8
American News	28	32	14
Anderson Clayton	43	35	−16
Avnet	40	57	43
Baker Oil Tools	18	21	17
Beatrice Foods	62	58	−6
Bemis Co.	47	49	4
Brown & Sharpe	34	27	−21
Brush Beryllium	40	33	−18
Bullard	38	41	8
Bunker Ramo	15	17	13
Chock Full O'Nuts	17	19	12
Cincinnati Milling	67	50	−25

GROUP V

Stock	Price 8/3/67	2/1/68	% Change
Acme Markets	39	37	−5%
Admiral	24	18	−25
Aerojet-General	30	25	−17
Allied Mills	48	46	−4
American So. African	44	61	39
American Zinc	21	23	10
Anchor Hocking	45	44	−2
Arden-Mayfair	13	13	0
Armstrong Cork	56	56	0
Santa Fe	30	28	−7
Bobbie Brooks	17	17	0
Braniff Air	68	42	−38
Brown Co.	19	23	21
Burlington Ind.	37	40	8
Campbell Red Lake	23	36	57

should outperform Group III stocks, and so on. Later on, we shall examine Value Line's claims more closely, but, for the present, let us choose the first fifteen from the Group I stocks listed in their weekly summary on August 11, 1967 (the date was picked at random) and the first fifteen stocks of Group V and see their performance over the next six months.

Prices have been adjusted to take stock dividends into account.

Let us now arrange the stocks in each group in decreasing order of the percentage changes in prices.

GROUP I		GROUP V	
Avnet	43%	Campbell Red Lake	57%
Am. Crystal Sugar	17	American So. African	39
Baker Oil Tools	17	Brown Co.	21
American News	14	American Zinc	10
Bunker Ramo	13	Burlington Ind.	8
Chock Full O'Nuts	12	Arden-Mayfair	0
Bullard	8	Armstrong Cork	0
Bemis Co.	4	Bobbie Brooks	0
Beatrice Foods	−6	Anchor Hocking	−2
Am. Machine & Foundry	−8	Allied Mills	−4
American Bakeries	−11	Acme Markets	−5
Anderson Clayton	−16	Santa Fe	−7
Brush Beryllium	−18	Aerojet-General	−17
Brown & Sharpe	−21	Admiral	−25
Cincinnati Milling	−25	Braniff Air	−38

Group I stocks have a higher percentage increase than their corresponding Group V stocks in seven instances—American News over American Zinc, Bunker Ramo over Burlington Ind., Chock Full O'Nuts over Arden-Mayfair, Bullard over Armstrong Cork, Bemis Co. over Bobbie Brooks, Brown & Sharpe over Admiral, and Cincinnati Milling over Braniff Air. A person without a system dividing this group of thirty stocks into two groups at random would easily get seven or more leads for one group of stocks over the other group of stocks.

The probability of producing seven or more leads by random selection is 56%, so that he would do it more than half the time. (See Appendix D for the method of calculation.) It is very likely, therefore, that anybody could produce seven or more leads from this group of stocks, and Value Line's performance here was not very good. However, we shall shortly see that Value Line's performance improves markedly when we consider larger samples, so that this small sample is nothing but a bad fluctuation which can happen to anybody.

Even if each of Value Line's Group I stocks had led each of the Group V stocks in the above example, anyone would have had a 6% chance of doing as well just by random selection from the thirty stocks. So while it is highly unlikely that a person selecting at random could perform this well, it is not impossible. Therefore, we have to accept the fact that there is always a chance that anybody, or any firm, claiming to have a valid system, is mistaken in that belief even if it works well over limited data. But, since we can never be absolutely certain of anything in this complex world of ours, no intelligent person considers any theory or system or dogma an absolute truth. People who claim to have "higher," "inner," "ultimate," or "whole" truths are living in a dream world, not the world of reality. Their kind of arrogance has no place in any scientific inquiry.

I am convinced there can be no sharp definitive division between believable and unbelievable systems, only a gradual melding of the reasonable into the unreasonable.

Very few investment services put their advice in a form appropriate for analysis of validity. Since The Value Line is one that does, we are able to analyze its results with much larger samples. For the periods with which we shall deal, Value Line always placed one hundred stocks in Group I, their predicted top performers, and one hundred stocks in Group V, their predicted worst performers. Analyzing their

48

predictions in the above manner using all Group I and all Group V stocks for many different time periods shows that Value Line actually has a system that discriminates among stocks. For example, if in the time period used above for the group of thirty stocks, all one hundred stocks in Group I are matched against all one hundred stocks in Group V, there is only a 6% chance of a person doing better than Value Line when choosing at random from these two hundred stocks. A study of twenty-five two hundred stock samples from Groups I and V shows an average of 8%, so that Value Line should do better in picking stocks ninety-two times in a hundred than a person picking at random.

But how can this be? Apparently, we had just got through showing that the public set the price of each stock in such a way that a 10% gain per year was to be expected and that no discrimination among stocks was possible. Now we discover that one of the investment advisory services very likely has a system for picking stocks that will do better than others. We shall resolve this paradox in the next two chapters when we delve into the factors that cause stock prices to change.

CHAPTER VI

THE PRINCIPLE OF MAXIMUM CONFUSION

"My kingdom for a horse."
SHAKESPEARE, *Richard III*

EACH one of us tries to achieve his goals in the way he thinks best. At the races, each bettor selects the horse he thinks will win. In the stock market, each investor buys stocks that he thinks will go up. In the market place, each consumer buys those goods that he thinks offer the best value. In politics, each citizen votes for those candidates he thinks will best serve his interests. A wide variety of opinion exists on all topics and that is hardly surprising, considering the diversity of people and interests. What is truly amazing is the way all these opinions jell—in the totalizator machines at the track, in Wall Street, in the various consumer goods markets, in the voting booth—into a final consensus that reflects and weighs in the best possible way all the factors involved. The race track and the stock market have thus far provided excellent examples of this wondrous process, and we shall consider this process again in our last chapter.

If the public acting collectively can anticipate racing results and stock prices as well, as shown in the last few chapters, how is it possible for any individual to do better? Of course, some people will be just plain lucky, but most will have the usual run-of-the-mill luck. Therefore, if they play the horses, in time they will lose the money they risk, and if they play the stock market, they will make about 10% per year on their money. The only way a person can do better is to be privy to and act on information that is available only to relatively few other people. Such information is known as a "tip" in most circles and has a bad connotation. Usually by the time a tip reaches you, it has had wide circulation, and if the information that set it off was valid, the information has been discounted and the price of the stock has changed—or the odds on the horse. The trick is to know, first, whether or not the tip came from a reliable source, and second, how widespread the tip's distribution, and third, what interpretation should be placed on it.

The basic principle that forms the foundation of the investing system of this book, the Principle of Maximum Confusion, is now proposed. It is that the public is only likely to err in appraising a situation when there exist factors of importance not immediately evident. Only when the public makes a mistake do more favorable opportunities to make money exist in the stock market. I was once hired by a company whose stock is listed on the American Stock Exchange as a consultant to develop for them a new type of radiation dosimeter. When I was convinced that the dosimeter was ready, I bought some stock in the company because the new product would be responsible for a nice earnings increase. The day the new dosimeter was announced, the stock went up 10%. Here was real, first-hand, inside information, the kind very few people are privileged to get. I knew of an important new factor in the company's situation and was almost alone in my knowledge before the public heard about the news and adjusted the price of the stock accordingly.

I originally introduced the Principle of Maximum Confusion in my book *Horse Sense* * and used it to formulate the first and only mathematically sound system for successful betting at the track. It was stated in somewhat different form there, and it is pertinent to see how it works out in horse betting. "The betting public is most likely to err in determining the winning probability of the favorite in those races where the past performance record of the favorite is very similar to that of one or more other horses in the race." For the races, the intuitive idea behind the principle is that although the favorite appears very much like the other horses in ability, there must be some reason or reasons not immediately obvious for the betting public to make that horse favored. Yet, because the two horses seem alike on the surface, the public may be confused enough to bet too heavily on the other horse, making the favorite underbet. For those unfamiliar with racing parlance, the favorite in a race is the horse on which the most money is bet. The same considerations apply if the record of the favorite is not as good as one or more other horses in the race, since the public must have some reason for making an apparently inferior animal the favorite. In the converse case where one horse, who will of course be the favorite, has a record outstanding in every respect relative to all the other horses in the race, it is certain that its outstanding qualifications will not be lost on the public. In all probability, this type of horse will be either overbet or properly bet, that is, anyone betting horses like these will lose 15% or more on the amount he bets. Using the Principle of Maximum Confusion, however, it is possible

* *Horse Sense: A New and Rigorous Application of Mathematical Methods to Successful Betting at the Track* by Burton P. Fabricand, published by David McKay Company, Inc., New York, 1965.

to bet just those few favorites that are underbet and realize almost a 30% profit on the amount wagered.

We have seen that in the stock market as at the race track, we are playing against other people. And the collective judgment of our opponents is excellent. Therefore, apply the Principle of Maximum Confusion to the stock market in order to discover significant unrecognized factors about any stock. Those stocks are apt to be underpriced. The key point, we shall see, is surprise. A sudden change in a company's prospects is usually discounted (that is, the stock's price will change) by the public only after a time lag, and profitable stock purchases can be made during this period of confusion.

Of course the small individual investor is at a disadvantage in the all important quest for timely investment information. Insiders and fund managers, who maintain good contacts with the officials of many companies, become aware of changes in company prospects early, and act on the information before any outsiders can. By the time the news is public, the stock has had its price move.

Two actions initiated in recent years by the Securities and Exchange Commission will help the small investor and tend to put him on a more equal footing with the officers, directors, and key employees of companies in obtaining information. (We shall presently see how significant these changes in the nature and handling of inside information are to the individual investor and why, in the future, the profitability of the stock selection system to be presented may be considerably enhanced.)

The first action by the Securities & Exchange Commission was the Texas Gulf Sulphur case. The Circuit Court of Appeals ruled that a group of the corporation's top officers had breached the law by buying TGS stock, "calls" on the stock, and accepting stock options, without disclosing what they knew about a huge copper, zinc, and silver discovery in Kidd

Township, Ontario. The initial ore discovery was made in November 1963. Its magnitude was not revealed to the public until April 16, 1964. As late as April 12, a press release from the company played down rumors of the great mineral find.

Between November and April, the officers concerned had bought 9100 shares of TGS in the open market, purchased calls on 5200 additional shares and were granted options in February 1964 to purchase 31,200 shares from the company treasury at just under $24 per share. "Tips" were also passed to other people, who bought 12,100 shares and also purchased calls on 14,100 shares. In all, about 70,000 shares of stock were involved. When the buying was going on, TGS stock fluctuated in the 24-30 range. One year later, the stock was around 70 and has since gone much higher. Thus, insider profits of several million dollars were made as the direct consequence of persons acting on secret and significant information not available to the public.

The second case was the S. E. C.'s proceeding against the large brokerage firm of Merrill Lynch, Pierce, Fenner and Smith, Inc. in August 1968. This case was different in that persons outside a company were charged with violations. In the Texas Gulf affair, only persons directly connected with the company were involved. The S. E. C. charged that Merrill Lynch and fourteen of its executives and salesmen committed fraud by furnishing information about an earnings decline at the Douglas Aircraft Company to fifteen investment companies before the information was made available to the public. The information enabled these large institutional clients to avoid losses by selling their Douglas shares, or to make profits by selling Douglas shares short (see Appendix E). Merrill Lynch had learned about the earnings decline at Douglas through its role as prospective managing underwriter for a Douglas issue of $75,000,000 in convertible debentures. In addition, according to the S. E. C., the use of the information by the investment companies constituted fraud, and such well-known concerns as the Dreyfus Corporation, A. W. Jones & Co., and the Madison Fund, as well as other large organizations, were charged with securities law violations. No charges were made against Douglas or any of its officers and directors.

The story of the investigation leading to the charges is interesting. On June 7, 1966, Douglas reported earnings of 85¢ a share in the five-month period ended April 30 of that year. A second report, issued on June 24, pointed to a drastic reversal in the company's fortunes. Earnings in the six-month period ending May 31 were placed at 12¢ a share and management expressed the opinion that Douglas might not even show a profit for the full fiscal year ending November 30, 1966. At some time during the period between June 17 and June 22, the S. E. C. charged, Merrill Lynch obtained the information that was to be released to the public on June 24 and passed it along to the fifteen institutions.

It was only some time later that the S. E. C.'s staff investigators became aware of this. What they did notice was a large increase in the volume of trading in Douglas shares on the New York Stock Exchange in the days just prior to the second earnings announcement. Computer runs on the Douglas trading showed that a substantial portion came from Merrill Lynch. Ordinarily, this is not significant because the concern is the nation's largest brokerage house and customarily accounts for large volume. However, the investigators knew of Merrill Lynch's involvement in the Douglas debenture underwriting and they decided to look further. Their investigations disclosed not only that the sellers were large institutional clients of Merrill Lynch but also that a substantial amount of short selling had taken place. Short selling is regarded as risky and is rarely indulged in by institutions. Subsequent investigations revealed that the group of institutions either sold or sold short a total of 190,000 Douglas shares between June 20 and

June 23, the day before public disclosure of the earnings decline.

On June 22, Douglas stock opened at 90½ and one week later, on June 29, it closed at 64⅜. The institutional clients of Merrill Lynch, according to the S. E. C., either avoided losses or made profits totaling as much as $4,500,000 during that period. At the same time, some of Merrill Lynch's salesmen were actually buying Douglas shares for other customers.

At issue in both cases is the right of the small investor to know as much as anybody else when he makes a securities transaction. If this is not the case, the privileged few can reap large profits at the expense of the many. This is, of course, what we hope to do legally in this book with the help of the Principle of Maximum Confusion. But a point underscored by the principle is never, never to underestimate the public. Good ideas and valuable information are the scarcest of commodities, and a great deal of grief can be avoided if a person continually asks himself why it is that he believes he knows something that nobody else knows whenever he attempts to profit from some action.

CHAPTER VII

EARNINGS CHANGES VS PRICE CHANGES

"Having thus exposed the far-seeing Mandarin's inner thoughts, would it be too excessive a labour to penetrate a little deeper into the rich mine of strategy and disclose a specific detail?"

ERNEST BRAMAH, *Kai Lung Unrolls His Mat*

COMMON stock investing is as much concerned with people as with stocks. In fact, the stocks are almost incidental, since the important thing is what people think of them. Many students of the stock market assume that stocks have an intrinsic or absolute value, entirely apart from anybody's opinion of them, and that sooner or later, the popular opinion will coincide with this "true" value. Maybe so. But the situation is different here from that prevailing in horse racing. At the races, the people express their opinion of each horse in terms of the odds. Then, a completely independent physical event, the race itself, takes place. Using the results of many races, the judgment of the people can be compared with physical reality, i.e., the race results.

With stocks, however, no true physical value ever manifests itself. It is always a question of the price people will pay for a stock. If an analyst recommends the purchase of a stock, he thinks it undervalued and believes that it will eventually be bid up by the public to reach what he considers the proper price. The fallacy here is that the public may not be any more ignorant of the prospects of the stock now than later. Granted there will be times when the analyst, like a prospector, will stumble over a find unknown and underpriced, but I am sure that just as many times the exact opposite holds true and he is saved by the favorable nature of the game. There seems to be no way of demonstrating any absolute criterion, or intrinsic value, apart from public opinion, that determines the worth of a stock. Value is subjective, something existing in each person's mind. To "first of all know value," as counseled by Charles H. Dow, the originator of the Dow Theory, or "to buy stocks when they are cheap and sell them when they are dear," as Baron Rothschild advised, is to imply that an accepted standard of value exists. But no operational definition of value, that is, a definition that shows in detail how it can be measured objectively, has ever been formulated by any economist. So we follow the lead of physics and the other branches of science, in which, no matter how deep and abstract a theory may be, there must be a recipe described in specific and precise terms for applying the theory to observed events if it is to be considered meaningful. Lacking such a recipe, we shall ignore intrinsic value. For us, value is price and price value.

The price of the stock of a company is usually considered to be largely determined by the earnings per share. If the earnings per share is multiplied by a number called the price-to-earnings ratio, we arrive at the price per share of stock. This is a very simple relationship, but it masks a huge amount of complexity. What earnings per share figure, for example, do you use? That for the last fiscal year, or that estimated for the year ending at some date in the future so that a guess of future earnings is involved? And what determines the price-to-earnings ratio?

We have seen that a stock on average will bring in about 10% a year. So, however the public figures out the proper earnings per share and price-to-earnings ratio to use, we know it does an excellent job. Of course, for some stocks, conditions may evolve that bring about a much higher return, while for others, the opposite may take place. But, in general, the public has already considered all the factors that influence the earnings per share and the price-to-earnings ratio and has set a price for a stock that takes into account all that can be known at any given time. Otherwise, the high 10% return could hardly be achieved.

For the time being, let us accept the market price of a stock as the fair price at the time, and let us inquire into how changes in price come about. Changes in stock prices arise from two different causes. The following relationship, derived in Appendix F, shows how price changes are connected with changes in earnings and price-to-earnings ratios. *The percentage change in the price of a stock equals the percentage change in the earnings per share plus the percentage change in the price-to-earnings ratio*. This equation will be of great significance to us.

We must now say what the earnings per share and the price-to-earnings ratio really mean. One interpretation might be that the earnings per share is the reported earnings for the last fiscal year. If such is the case, it is a known, fixed quantity and no allowance is made for any variation in it. Therefore, the percentage change in earnings will be zero. All variations in price would then be attributed to changes in the price-to-earnings ratio. This view seems unlikely since there is strong evidence that stocks respond sharply in price to earnings increases and decreases of significant proportions. Recently, for example, Rayette-Faberge disclosed June 1968 quarterly earnings of 19¢ per share against a generally expected 70¢. The stock fell seven points that day, from 60½ to 53½. Wide, sudden price changes like this on unexpected news of earnings are not uncommon.

More plausible is the interpretation that the earnings per share includes an estimate of the earnings covering some period in the future. As the estimates of expected earnings change in response to changes in world conditions, stock prices will fluctuate. In the case of Rayette-Faberge, the lower-than-expected earnings caused the investing public to lower sharply its earnings projections for the future for that stock, with the consequence that the value of the stock was greatly reduced.

It is true that nobody can forecast future earnings with pinpoint accuracy. But presumably the market makes some projection of earnings and sets the price of the stock accordingly, that is, by assigning some multiple to these earnings. When a company reports earnings at variance with the projection, the price of the stock will quickly adjust to the public's new view of reality. Here in the earnings projections lie many of the uncertainties in common stock investing, and also the opportunities for profit. If you as an investor have a better idea of what a company will earn in the future than anybody else, you will do better than others. If, on the other hand, your view of a company's prospects is faulty, you will probably do worse.

As an example, suppose the stock of the Bugjuice Corporation sells at $10 a share and suppose that the estimated earnings for the year ahead are suddenly increased by 10% from $1.00 per share to $1.10 per share because of a jump in the demand for frozen bug juice. If no change in the price-to-earnings ratio takes place, the price per share will increase from $10 to $11, or 10%. One never knows, of course, if the year ahead earnings are the proper figures to use. It may be that six months ahead or nine months ahead earnings are used by the market, or even some other amount. That depends on the stock in question. Still, there is little doubt that when the earnings projections are increased, the price of the stock will go up if there is no change in the price-to-earnings ratio. We will see this more clearly as we go on.

In this chapter, we shall assume that the price-to-earnings ratio remains constant for all time periods of concern to us so that all price changes come about because of changes in the earnings estimates. Admittedly, this is a great simplification. But we wish to examine the effect of considering only changes in earnings estimates. It turns out that this is almost all that we can use, or that we need because the price-to-earnings ratio is far too complex a quantity for anybody to handle adequately. Knowledge of changes in earnings estimates, coupled with the favorable nature of the game, is all that is needed to do very well indeed in the stock market.

On July 15, 1964, after the close of the market, Westinghouse Electric Corporation reported a sharp increase in earnings for the second quarter over the first quarter. The announcement caught Wall Street unawares. Everybody had been expecting a continuing decline in earnings from a corporation that had been experiencing difficulties, and no immediate turnaround was envisioned. The *New York Times* financial writer who reported this news even remarked in his article how surprising the higher earnings were. The next morning, Westinghouse opened on a block of 35,000 shares, up a point from the previous day. I myself purchased a substantial number of shares at the opening. For the next year, Westinghouse was one of the market's stellar performers, doubling in price in that time.

The unexpected earnings report caused analysts to revise their estimated earnings for Westinghouse sharply upward. And, therefore, the price of Westinghouse shares went up to take the new estimates into account. Surprise and confusion were the key to this situation. Those people who bought quickly got in before the news could be discounted in the price, and they reaped substantial profits. Much credit must go to the Westinghouse officers for keeping close-mouthed about the earnings report before its public release. In too many cases, information about earnings is old hat by the time the knowledge is made public, so that the stock has had its rise beforehand. Only insiders and their friends can benefit from information leaks of this sort. Actually, one never knows how much an earnings statement has affected prices of a stock before publication. In some instances, the price may go down on the announcement. Usually, however, an announcement of a surprising increase in earnings indicates that something good is going on in the company, something which analysts had heretofore not suspected. Proper discounting of the information may go on for six months or longer and the stock will continue to rise in price, especially if higher price-to-earnings ratios become warranted. Even though in these pages we are assuming no changes in price-to-earnings ratios, we must not forget that enhanced prospects for a company can be completely negated if a decreased ratio is assigned to the stock by the public as a result of other changes in the world situation.

Up till now, our underlying assumption has been that the market price for a stock is the fair price. The public has considered all the information available, projected some level of earnings, determined an appropriate multiple, and set stock prices to discount all possibilities. When the situation suddenly changes, as in the Westinghouse example, however, the public's price at that moment may not be the fair price. There may be a time lag before a proper price is determined. In such cases, we will see that this is the situation. Only when surprising changes occur in the conditions affecting stocks is there a chance to do better than the public, because the public lags in discounting the new information.

How does the individual investor know whether or not an

earnings statement is to be considered surprising? Reports on earnings are published every day, and, following each quarter, the number reaches flood proportions. The investor must do one of two things. Either he must analyze companies in sufficient depth to make earnings projections himself, or he must rely on professional analysts. The former way is much too time-consuming if one wants to cover a large number of companies, which one must do to get many plays of this sort. Unexpected earnings statements are not very common. Since there are many professional investment services that make estimates of projected earnings, why not use one? Then by comparing the actual earnings reported with the projections of the investment service, an unexpected earnings report can be noticed quickly. Of the many investment services, The Value Line Investment Survey should be singled out because it presents estimates on a regular basis for over 1400 companies.

As a rule of thumb, I consider an earnings statement "surprising" if it is over 10% higher than the estimate. An interesting case for me occurred September 1, 1967, when Avnet reported earnings of $2.33 for its fiscal year ending June 30 compared to a $2.00 expectation by many services. I bought at the opening the next day at 40. But, since the stock had been strong the previous week, I am sure that there had been a partial discounting of the news. The stock price did nothing for a week after I bought it, and then shot up to a high of 71 in the next three months.

It is more difficult to take advantage of a surprisingly low earnings announcement. On such occasions, the stock will open lower and continue on down in most instances. Since selling short must take place on an uptick in price and after all other sell orders, it is not easy to profit by this technique. Selling short in this inherently favorable game is fraught with danger, and it should not be attempted unless maximum advantage can be taken of the surprisingly low earnings.

Another method of investing profitably in stocks is to act when something happens in a company that causes analysts to revise their earnings estimates sharply upward. No actual earnings have to be reported. A case in point was Occidental Petroleum in the fall of 1965. Events transpiring in the company caused The Value Line to upgrade its estimates of company earnings, in a special supplementary report. Acting on this information, I bought the stock at 25 and saw it go to 57 within six months. The peak came when the president of the company, Dr. Armand Hammer, was written up in *Life* Magazine. By this time, it was of course too late for purchase since all the news and publicity that could possibly affect the stock for the near future had been disseminated.

Estimating earnings is a precarious business. Who can see very far into the future these days? Many times the analyst misinterprets data, or the assumptions on which he bases his estimates turn out all wrong, and he is far off in his predictions. Projections of sales and profit margins, the handling of such items as depreciation, taxes, inventory, non-recurring gains, and possible dilution by senior securities convertible into common stock, are all subject to widespread variations in interpretation. A good way to avoid many of these pitfalls is to follow the views of one analyst whose job it is to review a company regularly. It is likely that he will arrive at his earnings estimates in much the same way with every review, and the investor can depend on being alerted to all the important changes.

I have asserted in this chapter that price changes in stocks are largely tied to changes in earnings estimates. So it is necessary to set up some kind of demonstration to prove or disprove this statement. We shall proceed by noting two things: (1) the percentage change in estimated earnings for a corporation on a given date for the year ending six months in the future from the earnings estimated three months previously; and (2) the percentage change in actual price of the stock over the next three-month period. We hope to correlate these two numbers—if the percentage change in the earnings estimate is large, the price increase should be large, and if the percentage change in the estimate is small or nonexistent, the price change should be small.

Let's take some examples. On June 25, 1965, Value Line estimated that Polaroid would show earnings of $1.40 per share for the twelve months ending September 30, 1965. On September 24, 1965, the estimate was raised to $1.65 per share for the twelve months ending December 31, 1965. In the three-month period between June 25 and September 24, 1965, events were occurring in the company that caused the analyst to raise his estimate of earnings for Polaroid rather sharply, by 18%. The change in the estimated earnings per share was 25¢, from $1.40 to $1.65. If we divide 25¢ by the original estimate, $1.40, we get .18 or 18%. This change in estimate became evident to Value Line's subscribers on September 24, 1965, when the new estimate of $1.65 was published. The price of Polaroid on that day was 84, but three months later the price had risen to 127, a 52% advance. It can be assumed here that the public lagged in discounting Polaroid's rapidly improving prospects.

On April 30, 1965, the earnings of KLM Airlines for the year ending September 30, 1965, were projected at $2.50 by the Value Line analyst. Three months later, on July 30, the estimate was raised to $5.00 for the year ending December 31, 1965, an increase of 100%. The price on July 30 was 36, and three months later, on October 29, 1965, it was 68, a gain of 89%. Again, there seemed to be a lag in discounting improved prospects: the public was slow.

Matters do not always work out this well. On April 22, 1966, the earnings estimate for Ling-Temco-Vought was $3.95 per share for the year ending September 30, 1966. On July 22, 1966, this figure was raised to $4.75 for the year

65

ending December 31, 1966, an increase of 20%. But between July 22 and October 21, 1966, the price of Ling-Temco-Vought dropped from 62 to 43, a decline of 31%. This was a time of declining price-to-earnings ratios caused by the extremely tight money situation. The decline in the price-to-earnings ratio of Ling-Temco-Vought more than offset the expected improvement in the company's prospects. Three months after October 21, however, the price of the stock more than doubled, which indicates that there may be a lag greater than three months in discounting improved prospects. It depends on market conditions. Those people who held on through the tight money period reaped enormous profits in this stock.

Much has been said about the desultory performance of the blue chip sector in recent years. The performance of these stocks is no surprise when considered in the light of the principles expounded here. A typical case is that of Dupont. On February 10, 1967, the earnings estimate for the year ending June 30, 1967, was $7.85 per share. On May 12, 1967, it was $7.35 per share, a decline of 6%. The price on May 12 was 176 and on August 11, three months later, 156, a decline of 11%. Even though the market as a whole was rising strongly through this period, it failed to overcome Dupont's dull immediate prospects.

Merger prospects can also completely outweigh earnings projections. On July 22, 1966, the earnings per share for Douglas were estimated at zero for the year ending December 31, 1966, and on October 21, a whopping loss of $5.50 per share was predicted for the year ending March 31, 1967. Yet, from October 21, 1966 to January 20, 1967, the price of Douglas rose 31% from 36 to 47. During this time, the probability of a merger with McDonnell became apparent, which greatly enhanced Douglas' prospects.

Since The Value Line regularly reviews stocks every three months, it will be convenient to use their earnings estimates,

66

which are at least as good as those of anybody else. Selection of the year ending six months in the future for the time period of the earnings estimates is somewhat arbitrary, and other intervals like the next calendar year or the next nine months could also be used. However, the six-month period chosen yields the best results and, it is interesting to note, is also used by The Value Line in its system of stock selection. It would seem that the stock market likes to look ahead about six months on average to determine the prospects of stocks. Our program starts out with a big disadvantage because there can be up to a three-month delay before changes in earnings estimates by The Value Line become known. We shall see, even so, that good results are obtained.

We cover the three-year period from April 1965 to April 1968. All stocks for which The Value Line gave earnings estimates during that time are used, about 1000 in number. Since nobody to my knowledge has placed such emphasis on changes in estimated earnings in a consistent manner, I think it is worthwhile to exhibit some of the raw data from which my results arise. For each stock there is shown in the left hand column of the table below the date on which a new earnings estimate for the year ending six months in the future became available. In the left hand column under each stock, the percentage change in this estimate from that given three months earlier appears. In the right hand column under each stock, the percentage change in price over this three-month period is shown.

Thus, on September 3, 1965, Value Line raised its estimated earnings for Avnet by 9% over that from three months earlier. On December 3, 1965, the earnings estimate was unchanged, which is shown by 0%. On March 4, 1966, the estimate was jumped by 21% from that made on December 3, 1965. A minus sign in front of the estimate indicates a reduction. The abbreviation Inf. under Bunker Ramo means infinity. The

	Avnet		Burndy		Bunker Ramo		Collins Radio		Fairchild Camera	
9/3/65	9%	−7%	28%	22%	35%	−23%	19%	28%	22%	54%
12/3/65	0	29	20	61	9	17	33	41	36	80
3/4/66	21	6	5	16	−15	13	12	33	15	58
6/3/66	0	0	19	0	44	−7	3	−10	15	−26
9/2/66	31	−11	16	4	100	−6	5	8	14	23
12/2/66	5	−6	11	−7	Inf.	−20	16	−13	−17	−47
3/3/67	5	44	4	48	0	50	10	29	4	63
6/2/67	5	52	−2	−8	50	22	1	27	2	−4
9/1/67	11	3	−10	3	0	9	−1	4	−12	−18
12/1/67	33	70	−5	9	133	8	5	−7	−45	17
3/1/68		−19		−18		15		−22		−34

original estimate on September 2, 1966 was for zero earnings, so that any increase in this estimate involves a division by zero, which gives infinity.

In a similar manner, the price of Avnet went up 29% between September 3, 1965 and December 3, 1965. By March 4, 1966, it had appreciated another 6%.

The two numbers we wish to consider are the percentage change in earnings estimates on a given date, with the percentage change in price over the next three months. With Avnet, for example, the percentage change in the earnings estimate on September 3, 1965 was 9%—the estimate was raised 9% by The Value Line from its review three months earlier. Following the publication of this change, the price of Avnet shares appreciated 29% over the period to December 3, 1965. On December 1, 1967, the projection of the earnings of Bunker Ramo were raised 133% over the projection from three months previously, and the price appreciated 15% over the next three months to March 1, 1968.

The average appreciation for all stocks for all three-month intervals during the three-year period under consideration was 3.3%. This amounts to about 14% per year appreciation for the average stock. When dividends are added, the return for this three-year period was indeed substantial. We now wish to see if we can group all the stocks in such a way that those with the greatest changes in estimated earnings also have the greatest price increases, those with the smallest changes in estimated earnings the least price increases. In Group A will be all stocks for which the earnings estimate for the year ending six months in the future has been raised 10% or more by The Value Line since its review three months earlier. Group B will be composed of stocks for which the earnings estimate has been raised in the range five to nine percent, and Group C will consist of stocks for which the change in estimates is less than five percent. The percentage increase in price for the three

69

months following the change in estimates is averaged for all stocks in each of the three groups. The results are shown in the table.

	Percentage increase in estimates	Average 3-month percentage change in price	Number of 3-month intervals
Group A	10% or more	6.9%	1550
Group B	5% to 9%	3.8%	1637
Group C	4% or less	2.5%	7015
All stocks		3.3%	10202

The hoped-for difference among stocks does appear. Stocks in Group A appreciated an average of 6.9% in the three months following the sharp jump in estimated earnings. Compounded quarterly to find the yearly rate, the gain amounts to almost 31% per year on the amount invested. Note that this group included only 15% of the total number of three-month intervals. Group B stocks did second best, with an average three-month appreciation rate of 3.8%, or 16% per year. Only 16% of the total number of three-month intervals comprised this group. By far the largest number of intervals appears for Group C stocks. These stocks are judged to have little prospect for earnings appreciation. Even these stocks appreciated over the three-year period by an average of 2.5% every three months, or over 10% per year. It would seem that over the three-year period 1965 to 1968, almost everybody who owned stocks did very well indeed. Do not forget that this period included a widespread market decline in 1966. Such data add further evidence in favor of the hypothesis that the stock market is a favorable game.

There would seem to be no great mystery why some stocks do better than others: it is largely geared to earnings prospects. Forget pseudo-scientific considerations of business cycles and chart patterns. And forget astrology, Zen, voodoo, and all other mysticism. Forget also the sophisticated mathematical

70

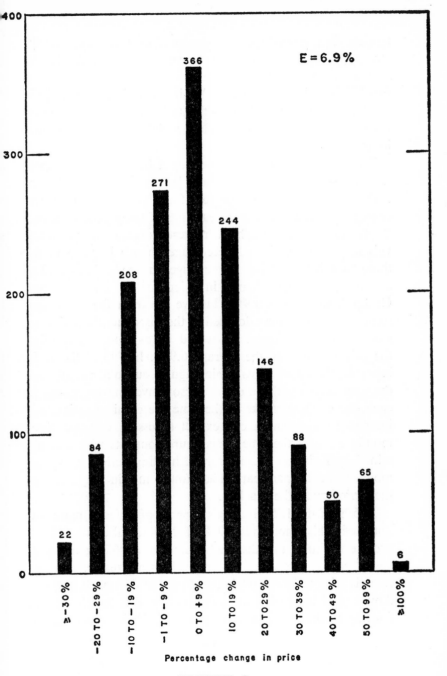

FIGURE 3

models, like those based on the random walk and relative strengths, which have little to do with the real stock market. People simply want those stocks that have good, and improving, earnings prospects. An investigation of any good stock market system will show this to be the key point, and all the rest is just so much camouflage which probably does more harm than good.

The distribution of the three-month intervals with respect to their respective percentage gains is interesting to see. Figure 3 shows the pattern for all stocks for which there was a percentage increase in estimated earnings of ten percent or more, the Group A stocks. Each bar represents the number of intervals having the indicated percentage change in price in the three months following the change in the estimates. The average percentage change in price for all intervals from Group A stocks was 6.9%, but we see from the graph that some stocks more than doubled in the three months and some stocks had sharp losses. As would be expected, most often the gain was around the average 6.9%. In 585 of the 1550 intervals, there was a loss, which figures out to about 38% of the total number. Therefore, a person investing his money in each one of these stocks at the time the earnings estimate is jumped 10% or more can expect a loss in the next three months 38% of the time. This figure contrasts with that obtained by Fisher and Lorie for all holding periods from one month to thirty-four years. They found that in only 22% of the periods was there a loss.

In 599 of the 1550 intervals a profit of 10% or more was obtained. This amounts to 39% of the intervals. Now a 10% profit every three months is equivalent to a 46% gain on invested capital per year. This represents a sizeable gain and there is a high 39% probability of getting this much or more. Any way of improving these figures would indeed be adding frosting to the cake. In seventy-one of the intervals a profit

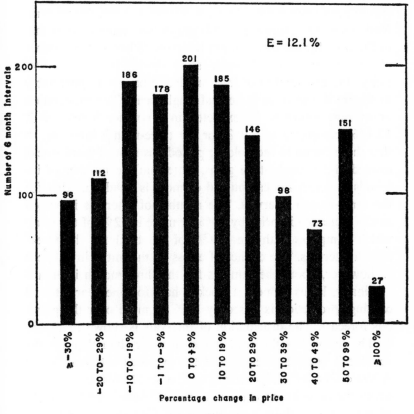

FIGURE 4

of 50% or more on the investment was obtained. This is 4½% of the total number of intervals.

Suppose a stock is held for six months after its earnings projection is raised by 10% or more. Let us take a look at the distribution of six-month intervals with respect to their respective percentage gains in price. Figure 4 shows this pattern. Notice how the character of this graph has changed from that in Figure 3 for the three-month intervals. Whereas the number of intervals in Figure 3 peaks rather sharply in the 0 to 9% range, the distribution of intervals has broadened appreciably in Figure 4 and there is no real single peak. The expectation or average return to be expected in a six-month interval is 12.1%, compared to 6.9% for the three-month intervals, so that the increase in the holding period has moved more stocks toward higher percentage gains. Note that the number of intervals in which stocks doubled or more is quadruple that for the three-month intervals. The number of intervals in which stocks increased in price by 50% or more is 12% of the total, which compares with the 4½% of the total for the three-month intervals. The chance of a loss on the initial investment is, however, about the same as for the three-month intervals.

Finally, let us suppose a stock is held for one year after its earnings projection is raised by 10% or more over the previous forecast. The distribution of intervals is shown in Figure 5. The graph has flattened out even more than that for the six-month holding periods, and the expected return is 34%. A loss on the initial investment was incurred 36% of the time, about the same as in the previous cases. There is a 6% chance of more than doubling your money (78 intervals out of a total of 1294) and an 18% chance of increasing it by 50% or more. In 50% of the intervals, the original investment increased by 10% or more. Don't forget that dividends have not been taken into consideration in the results depicted in Figures 3, 4, 5, and 6. These would have the effect of shifting

74

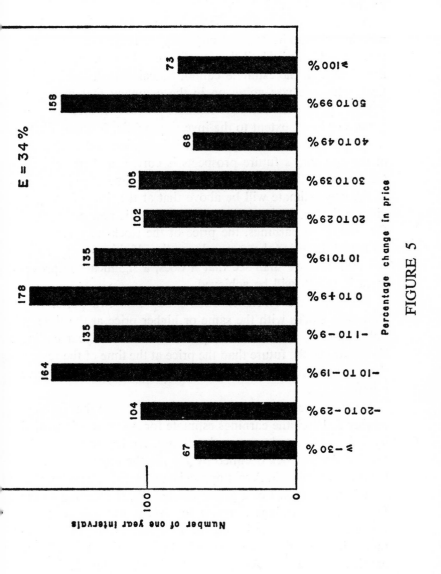

FIGURE 5

all dividend paying stocks towards higher percentage returns on the invested capital.

As I mentioned before, there can be a delay of up to three months before The Value Line's new earnings estimate for a stock is published. Until the new figure is known, the percentage change in the estimate cannot be calculated. During this time, whatever was going on in the company that made the analyst upgrade his earnings estimate probably leaked out to a greater or lesser extent to the investing public. It seems likely, therefore, that if the analyst's new information and evaluation of the company's future prospects is correct and not too far off the mark, the price of the stock at the time of publication of the new estimate will be above that at the time of the previous estimate. If the analyst is wrong in his new estimate of the company's earnings, the price of the stock may very well be below the price three months earlier. If this theory proves out well, and we shall see that it does, a significant improvement in results will be achieved.

We divide the stocks in each group into two parts. One shows the stocks with the same or higher price at the time of publication of the new earnings estimate for the year ending six months in the future than the price at the time of the review three months earlier, the other part shows the stocks that have a lower price.

If we go back to the table of raw data, we see that on September 3, 1965, the earnings estimate for Avnet was increased by 9% over that three months earlier. During this time, the price of Avnet stock declined by 7%. In the three months following September 3, Avnet appreciated by 29%. The number 29 will then be part of a group labeled Bb, B referring to the fact that the earnings estimate for Avnet was raised in the range 5% to 9%, and b to the fact that during this three-month interval, the price declined. On September 1, 1967, the earnings estimate for Avnet was raised 11%, while during the

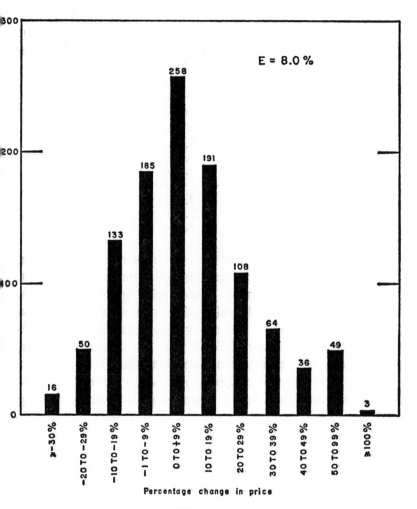

FIGURE 6

three months up to September 1, the price of the stock went up 3%. In the following three months the price increased 70%. The number 70 would then go into group Aa, A denoting an increase in estimated earnings by 10% or more and a an increase in price during that three-month period. The average results for each group follow.

	Average 3-month percentage change in price	Number of 3-month intervals
Group Aa	8.0%	1093
Group Ba	4.8%	1057
Group Ca	2.7%	3764
Group Ab	4.4%	457
Group Bb	2.0%	580
Group Cb	2.2%	3251

Those stocks whose prices increased or remained the same during the three-month interval in which the earnings estimate was changed show much greater price appreciation in the following three months, after the estimate is made public. Stocks in Group Aa had an average appreciation of 8.0% every three months, or 36% per year, a truly amazing return. Compare this figure to the lower but still substantial 4.4% every three months for Group Ab, which amounts to 19% per year. And these figures represent price appreciation only. Adding in dividends will increase the percentage return on investment by about 3% a year. Groups Ba and Ca also show price increases that are respectively higher than Groups Bb and Cb, indicating that an increase in projected earnings accompanied by rising prices are two important factors to look for when buying a stock.

The distribution of three-month intervals for the stocks of Group Aa is shown in Figure 6. It is similar to that of Figure 3 for Group A stocks. In 384 of the total number of 1093 intervals, there was a loss on the investment. This amounts to 35% of the total number and is somewhat less than for Group A stocks. The rather high chances of a loss for the Group A and Group Aa stocks comes about because the price of many stocks have risen, discounted in accordance with their new earnings estimates, before The Value Line could publish the revisions. Thus, by the time the new estimates appeared, the stocks were at their highs for the next three months or so.

While the data of Lorie and Fisher show that the average stock can be expected to yield about a 10% return on capital per year, we now have seen that stocks respond strongly to changes in earnings estimates over short periods of time, generally several months. The number of stocks showing large changes in earnings estimates is always a small part of the total number of stocks, and they get lost in the masses of statistics. They must be brought out of the confusion in the manner I have described here to be visible to the average investor. While many investors are aware that estimated earnings are important for predicting price behavior of stocks, there has been, to my knowledge, no previous systematic attempt to correlate changes in estimated earnings with price action.

The paradox with which I closed the last chapter can now be resolved if The Value Line's pick of the best acting stocks, those in Group I, include most of the stocks that have projected earnings increases of 10% or more. This is indeed the case. Over 95% of those stocks showing these sharp increases in estimated earnings for the year ending six months in the future fall into The Value Line's Groups I, II, and III. According to The Value Line, Group I stocks should act better than Group II stocks over the next year, Group II stocks should act better than Group III stocks, and so on. Suppose we pick a one-year period at random and compare the performance of the stocks in The Value Line's five identified groups with the actual performance of stocks chosen only on Value Line's estimated earnings. The latter we will organize into five groups, comprised of the following divisions: Group I—earnings estimates for the following year raised 20% or more; Group II—earnings estimates for the following year raised 10 to 19%; Group III—earnings estimates raised 1 to 9%; Group IV—earnings estimates raised 0%; Group V—earnings estimates reduced. The period chosen is from October 23, 1964 to January 15, 1965. During this span of time, Value Line made new earnings projections for all the stocks it reviews and placed them in one of its five groups. I have taken each stock and placed it in one of the five groups which we have based solely on changes of the earnings projections. The average change in price over the next one-year period was then calculated for each group, and the results are shown in the following table:

	Price appreciation for Value Line groups	Price appreciation for groups based on changes in estimates
Group I	27%	40%
Group II	13%	30%
Group III	13%	15%
Group IV	13%	16%
Group V	14%	15%

In both cases, Group I stocks did best, Value Line's Group I stocks appreciating an average 27% over the following year and my Group I an average of 40%. After Group I, any correlation between group rating and stock performance disappeared for Value Line, but persisted into Group II of my rankings. The probable reason that the performance of Value Line's Group I stocks is inferior to my Groups I and II is that Value Line includes in Group I too many stocks that do not show large jumps in earnings estimates, but that appear in Group I because by Value Line's criteria they are undervalued.

To summarize, the public generally evaluates each stock so that a 10% return on investment is to be expected per year, approximately. But, in those cases where a sharp earnings improvement becomes manifest, the public lags, opening the door to large profits for discerning investors who realize prices will rise because of the company's improved prospects.

One point more remains to be mentioned. It concerns the significance of the results obtained in this chapter. Earlier in the chapter, you remember, I divided stocks into three groups, A, B, and C. Group A stocks had an average three-month percentage appreciation of 6.9%, Group B stocks 3.8%, and Group C stocks 2.5%. The separation into three groups was based on the hypothesis that those stocks for which a large increase in estimated earnings was postulated by the analyst would appreciate in price the following three months to a greater extent than other stocks. Let us adopt the contrary hypothesis: imagine there is no information available at any given time that would enable a person to say that one stock will do better than another over some future time interval. This is the "random walk" model of the stock market. On this model, what chance does a person have of getting the above results for the three groups? We need not go into the details, but the proper statistical test to apply is the "t" test for the significance of the difference of two averages. This test indicates that on the basis of this hypothesis, a person would have only one chance in a hundred of obtaining the above results by pure luck. In other words, it is extremely unlikely that anyone could discriminate among stocks this well without the use of some system or legerdemain. The evidence for a system based on changes in earnings estimates is overwhelming.

CHAPTER VIII

PRICE-TO-EARNINGS RATIOS

When in doubt, be bullish.

HOW much are you willing to pay for each dollar of earnings of a company? If the company sells a product like an electronic computer whose sales are bound to increase over the years no matter what the economic situation, you will most likely pay a lot. Such is the case for International Business Machines stock, where you pay about fifty dollars for each dollar of earnings. On the other hand, if the company sells cod liver oil, the market for which is small and decreasing, you will pay very little for each dollar of earnings. The amount paid for each dollar of earnings is just the price-to-earnings ratio. It represents an appraisal by the investor of the fair present price to pay for a company's prospects.

Many, many factors go into the price-to-earnings ratios assigned to common stocks in the stock market. I will discuss some of them here. The great diversity and apparent inconsistencies in the ratios are sometimes surprising. Rather than trying to derive price-to-earnings ratios from fundamental information, initially, I am assuming that the investing public is as aware as anyone of the factors influencing the stock

82

market and puts the best possible value on the ratio for each stock. Let us then see what causes the ratio to change.

We begin by considering a simple model, a stock market sealed so that money can neither enter through the purchase of stocks nor leave through the selling of stocks. If shares are bought by an investor, an equivalent dollar amount of shares must be sold, and if shares are sold, an equivalent dollar amount of shares must be bought, so that the total amount of money in the market remains constant. The price of an average share of stock would be given by the total amount of money in the market divided by the total number of shares. Since both the total amount of money and the number of shares are fixed, the price of the average share of stock cannot change. The price-to-earnings ratio of the average share, which is obtained by dividing the price of the average share by the average earnings of all companies, must vary inversely with the average earnings. If corporate earnings are in a generally rising trend, the average price-to-earnings ratio in this kind of market will decline, and if corporate earnings are in a falling trend, the average price-to-earnings ratio will increase. Overall, then, any changes in earnings will be negated by opposing changes in the price-to-earnings ratios, leaving the price of the average share of stock unchanged.

This model of the market may not sound very realistic. But the real stock market seems to approximate it at times. From 1945 to 1950, the market showed steadily declining price-to-earnings ratios as corporate earnings advanced and prices did nothing.

Of course, for an individual stock in this simple model of the market, any price-to-earnings ratio is possible. Those stocks with assured and strongly rising earnings will attract attention and will sell at higher price-to-earnings ratios than the others. If a company enhances its prospects by developing a new product or process, or by a possible merger, or by the

83

discovery of a large natural resource deposit, it will attract money away from other stocks. Conversely, if a company loses a monopoly or a patent runs out or earnings decline, it will lose investor interest to more favorably situated stocks.

The point to keep in mind about this stock market model is that for every investor who makes a dollar, another investor must lose a dollar. Otherwise, the total amount of money in the market could not stay fixed. On this model, the stock market is not a favorable game, which I have defined as one in which *all* investors are more likely to win than lose. Here, each investor is just as likely to lose as win. If we make the model a little more realistic by allowing for commissions, the model becomes an unfavorable game, since there is a continual drain of money into the hands of the brokers. Obviously, then, this model does not correspond very closely to the actual stock market where all the players are more apt to win than lose, especially if long periods of time are considered.

The above example illustrates how price-to-earnings ratios may vary with earnings when the total amount of money available for investment in common stocks stays relatively constant. For short periods of time, such a condition may exist in the actual market. But the stock market is in continual competition with all other forms of investment for the public's money. Also, the total amount of money in circulation increases steadily as our economy grows, and some of this money flows into the stock market. Therefore, it is much more probable that the total amount of money in the stock market increases with time, although there may be some periods when it stays the same or decreases. If the supply of common stock fails to grow as rapidly as the money available for investment in the stock market, stock prices must rise. Here is the reason why stock prices have in general gone up since the dawn of stock market history, why all investors are more likely to win than lose, and why there does not have to be a loser for every winner.

Here too, in the money supply, we find an added complication as we try to predict changes in the price-to-earnings ratios. The more money put into the stock market, the higher stock prices will be and price-to-earnings ratios. The less money put into stocks, the lower stock prices and price-to-earnings ratios will be. Overall, changes in the prices of stocks because of changes in the money supply will occur independently of earnings changes, and they are due to changes in the price-to-earnings ratios.

During the period 1946 to 1949, the dividend return on equities was extraordinarily high compared to yields on fixed income securities. So great was the spread that the laws governing investments by personal trust funds, life insurance companies, and mutual savings banks were revised to allow the purchase of common stocks. In addition, mutual and pension funds began to enjoy increasing popularity. Huge amounts of money entered the stock market and drove price-to-earnings ratios considerably higher. The additional money, together with a strongly rising trend in corporate earnings, led to the great bull market of the 1950s. Today, there is a continuing upward pressure on the prices of the rather limited supply of common stocks. This pressure is the result of the purchases of the multitude of institutional and pension funds, which have lots of money to invest. There is also a steadily increasing interest in the stock market by many people just becoming aware of the favorable nature of the game.

Spotting changes in the total amount of money earmarked for investment in common stocks is a hard problem. You must note, as a bare minimum, the following factors: (1) the liquidity of the funds; (2) the flow of funds to institutional investors, who may or may not commit funds to common stocks; (3) the amount of savings; (4) Federal Reserve Board policy with respect to stock margin requirements and the money supply; (5) the yields on other forms of investment, like bonds and savings accounts; (6) the attractiveness of stocks to foreign investors since there is a large and increasing number of dollars to be found outside the country.

It should be evident that trying to forecast changes in price-to-earnings ratios is rather hopeless. There are too many complex, interacting variables, none of which can be measured accurately. Over the period 1926 to 1960, when the average return on stocks was about 9% per year compounded annually, the yield on high-grade bonds averaged about 4%. Lately, bond yields have been two or three percentage points higher, and one might think that the increased competition for the dollar offered by bonds should depress the prices of common stocks. At times, this undoubtedly happens. And at times, other of the above factors assume more importance. For example, in the spring of 1968, the stock market made a big rally in the face of very high interest rates because of the large amount of money in the hands of the funds and foreign investors that was committed to common stocks. Not nearly enough is known at present to predict just what a simple change in bond yields, as compared to stock yields, will do to stock prices. Those analysts who continually harp on the importance of the relative yields of stocks and bonds should look a little deeper into the problem.

Not all stocks will rise and fall an equal amount when the general economic barometers mentioned before cause the average of all prices to change. When the market as a whole is rising, some securities will advance much more rapidly than the average, and others will move against the trend and actually decline. When the market as a whole is declining, some securities will go down much faster than average, while others will move against the trend and rise. Many times, this contrary action by certain stocks is caused by sharply changed earnings estimates, but changes in the price-to-earnings ratio for the individual companies may also be important. Events within specific industries, as they affect specific companies, must be taken into account in forecasting the price-to-earnings ratios, in addition to the more general factors already discussed. Have the pospects of a company been changed by new developments in the whole industry, or by a change of company management or new management policies, or by new discoveries and new products?

In view of the enormous complexity underlying the price-to-earnings ratio, what can be made of the numerous models conjured up by analysts to determine the proper price to pay for a security? At the risk of offending many security analysts, the answer would have to be not much. Their models, no matter how mathematical they may be, must be recognized as just models, and any relation to the real stock market is purely coincidental. Still, making models does serve a purpose. It enables one to get a handle on the real thing so as to be able to think about it. I have no doubt that the better analysts realize the immense complication with which they must cope, and recognize the limitations of their methods. Benjamin Graham, the founder of scientific security analysis, constantly emphasizes the difficulties inherent in that field. Similar problems are shared by scientists in all areas. Even in physics, the most advanced of the sciences, where the phenomena treated succesfully are orders of magnitude simpler than the stock market, the correspondence between model and reality is open to serious question in many, many instances.

Let us take a look at the basic procedure used to estimate a stock's worth. Whether or not you are aware of it, you go through this process every time you buy a security, although in a more qualitative and fuzzy way. Suppose the stock of XYZ Corporation sells at $10.00 per share and that it earned $1.00 per share in its last fiscal year. You wish to know if the stock is worth what the market says. Or, putting it another way, you wish to know if the future income benefits to be derived from owning this stock are fully reflected in the present price.

To begin, you try to estimate the growth rate of XYZ's earnings. You consider the probable future course of the economy, guess the company's sales and profit margin in this context, consult your favorite fortune-teller, and finally decide that XYZ's earnings will grow at the rate of 5% per year compounded annually for the next ten years. This means that the company will earn five percent more this year than last year, or $1.05 per share for the present fiscal year. Next year it will earn five percent more than $1.05, or $1.1025, and so on for ten years. At the end of that time, the company will show earnings of $1.63 per share. (The mathematical manipulations for deriving the present worth of a company's stock are given in Appendix G.)

Next, you must forecast what multiple on these earnings will be applied by the stock market ten years from now, to determine the price of the stock then. You gaze into your crystal ball and come up with ten times, the same as the present price-to-earnings ratio. The stock will then sell at $16.30 per share ten years from now, a 63% increase over the present price.

Finally, you must decide what rate of return per annum on your original investment represents a fair return. You consider the prevailing level of interest rates and what their most likely future course will be, the world economic and political situation, and your horoscope, and you say you would like 9% per year, the same return yielded by stocks over the period 1926 to 1960. So you then must calculate what the present price of the stock should be if it is to grow to $16.30 in ten years if there is a 9% increase in it each year. It turns out that under the conditions assumed above, the price to pay for the stock today is $6.875 per share. This price represents the proper value of the stock, in your opinion, so the present market price of $10.00 per share makes the stock overpriced.

This is the procedure used by analysts to determine "true" value. Some analysts use dividends instead of earnings in their calculations, and others use a combination of both. But note the very far-reaching assumptions made. First, there is the estimated growth rate in earnings far into the future. Second, there is the capitalization to be applied to future earnings by the stock market of the future. And third, there is the discount to the present of future value. All such reasoning must be considered nothing but rank speculation. The public as a whole does the same thing when the market prices for stocks are set in the market place. And from all that can be shown up to the present time, the public, over long periods of time, does this at least as well as any individual.

We see that the "proper" price to pay for a stock depends on (1) the growth rate in earnings, (2) the future price-to-earnings ratio assigned to the stock by the market, (3) the fair return to be expected on an investment in common stocks, and (4) the number of years into the future the investor projects his figures. All these quantities can be juggled by the analyst to arrive at almost any price he desires. There are some restraints, however. For instance, if a high growth rate in earnings is assumed, the number of years over which this growth can be maintained must be limited. If a 20% growth rate in earnings is projected for the next hundred years for a company earning $1.00 per share today, the earnings one hundred years from now would come to almost $100,000,000 per share. Capitalized at ten times, each share of the company would sell for one billion dollars. Supposing the company had ten million shares outstanding, its worth in the marketplace would be ten million billion dollars, which seems like an impossible amount, even for the computer stocks of the future. The present gross national product is just under one thousand billion dollars, and assuming a 4% growth rate for the next hundred years gives a GNP then of about fifty thousand billion dollars, less than our hypothetical company's worth.

Let us, as an actual example, apply the foregoing procedure to International Business Machines, which is perhaps the leading glamor stock and sells at a very high price-to-earnings ratio. In 1967, IBM earned $5.00 per share. Let us forecast a 15% growth rate in earnings for the next ten years, which seems a reasonable projection based on present knowledge. If we assume that the earnings ten years from now will be capitalized at forty times, a norm from the past, and that future value will be discounted at 9%, the "proper" price to pay for these shares now is $337.50 per share. This "proper" price is actually close to the market price at the present time. Such agreement in price, however, must be regarded as accidental because of the amount of guesswork involved. What is interesting to note in the case of IBM is that the high current price-to-earnings ratio assigned by the stock market to IBM shares can be justified by very reasonable assumptions as to IBM's growth rate. Never let a high price-to-earnings ratio in itself deter you from buying a stock.

In summary, changes in the price-to-earnings ratio are the result of very complex happenings occurring worldwide. If anyone is under the illusion that he can understand these events and, more importantly, understand how people will interpret them, he is welcome to predict changes in the price-to-earnings ratios and test his forecasts in the market with his money. As for the rest of us mortals, we shall recognize the inherently "bullish" nature of the stock market and not try to gauge the fluctuations in price-to-earnings ratios. Sooner or later, price-to-earnings ratios will be established that reward our emphasis on earnings changes handsomely.

CHAPTER IX

THE MANAGEMENT OF PORTFOLIOS I. CAPITAL GAINS FOR THE AGGRESSIVE INVESTOR

Margin, Margin
How I love you,
How I love you,
My dear old Margin.

JULIAN STONE

I HAVE the privilege and responsibility of advising many friends and relatives on the management of their portfolios. I do this in accordance with the principles discussed in the previous chapters as well as the needs and objectives of the individual person. To illustrate with practical applications, I shall discuss three types of portfolios, one for capital gains, one for a combination of capital gains and moderate income, and lastly, one for income primarily and capital gains secondly. These three types pretty much exhaust the possibilities. The construction of portfolios for capital gains and large income together runs counter to the probabilities that exist in the stock market. We have seen that the average return to be expected on common stocks from appreciation in price and dividends is about 10% per year. Therefore, a stock having a high

91

dividend yield is not expected to appreciate in price as much as a stock not paying any dividend, and a stock paying no dividend is expected to reward its holder by going up in price to a greater extent than dividend paying stocks. At one end of the spectrum, we have stocks with low yields and higher probabilities of price appreciation. At the other end, we have stocks with high yields and limited expectations of price increases. In between, there are stocks with moderate yields and moderate probabilities for price appreciation.

Two factors affecting the price of a stock are, we have seen, changes in the estimates of future earnings and changes in the price-to-earnings ratios. So complicated are the variables entering into the latter quantity that attempts at predicting changes in it are futile considering the present state of knowledge. Accordingly, we will consider instead that we live in a country with the greatest economy ever seen. Investment in the shares of American corporations provides an unparalleled opportunity for capital growth. Temporary disruptions in the economy will occur of course, and capital values will suffer for short terms. But I see no reason not to trust the American people to choose political leaders who, acting together with our constantly improving level of corporate managers, are able to deal effectively with any economic problem that may arise. The odds are heavily in favor of a constantly growing economy, and the chances of another catastrophe, such as the one in 1929, are quite low.

As far as changes in the price-to-earnings ratios are concerned, then, we will always take a bullish posture. That is, we shall manage our portfolios under the assumption that price-to-earnings ratios will stay about the same or increase in the future, and we will rely on the favorable nature of the game to carry us through the inevitable uncertainties and fluctuations. The process of portfolio selection then devolves down to spotting as quickly as possible changes in the earnings estimates of corporations. For the aggressive investor willing and able to watch the stock market on a full-time basis, it means keeping eyes and ears open, being constantly alert to all estimates and earnings reports. The Value Line Investment Survey, because it regularly reviews and projects earnings for over 1400 stocks, is a very handy tool. Also very useful is Standard & Poor's Earnings Forecaster which compiles earnings estimates for many corporations from various sources.

We will assume that a stock gives a signal for making an investment when we see the following three circumstances: (1) An analyst whose earnings estimates you watch closely suddenly upgrades his forecast for a company by 10% or more, with his previous and new predictions covering the same period; (2) The officers themselves enlarge estimates of their company's prospective earnings by 10% or more, the previous and new predictions covering same period; (3) The actual earnings reported are 10% or more greater than that forecast by the analyst or by the company officers for the period.

Note that we are not interested in comparing the earnings for the present period of time with the corresponding period last year. Such a comparison is already taken into account in the forecasts by the analyst or company officials, and has already been long discounted by the market.

There are many, diverse reasons for changes in estimates. An investor may be able to analyze events, as reported by the news services, well enough to translate them into new earnings estimates before the analyst does. Mergers, new products, technological changes, new natural resource discoveries are some possibilities. In the late summer of 1967, I awoke to what the steadily rising prices for silver would do for the earnings of silver miners like Sunshine Mining. Fantastic earnings increases seemed assured, and yet the price of the stock had done very little. I bought in heavily, and within six months the stock doubled. There is an interesting point to be made here. When

I am interested in a stock, I always ask various brokers and investors what they think of it. Those stocks which are well-known and about which I receive favorable comment—stocks with a "following," as they say—more often than not have smaller price rises than stocks about which little is known or the comment is actually negative. Sunshine Mining, for example, received non-committal or unfavorable comment, and one advisory service had it at the head of its short sale list.

Stocks with a "following" have few secrets. Many fund managers and analysts have developed close relationships with corporate managements of popular companies over the years. As large shareholders, and representatives of large shareholders, they are treated with respect and consideration. Information is passed to them which can be acted on quickly before it is readily available to you or me as an individual investor. By the time we are able to buy, the stock has probably had an initial move, thereby cutting into our potential percentage gain.

Do not expect your interpretation of earnings reports and other events to coincide with that of the market in every case. Too much can go wrong in making an earnings estimate, and your analyst's figures or your figures may not be what the market is projecting at the time. Or the market may have already discounted your information. Or again, your interpretation and figures may be right, but a general change in price-to-earnings ratios may be taking place which vitiates your price expectations. In 1966, during that long downtrend in stock prices, unexpectedly good earnings reports did occur, but they had little effect on prices. High interest rates and tight money were overwhelming in their action. But overall, your results should be very much superior to the market averages.

Among the stocks for which higher earnings have been forecast, there does not seem to be any precise way to pick those that will do best, or to assign different probabilities of price increases to them. Therefore, diversification of one's portfolio is a necessity in order to achieve a return on capital near the average. Of course, an investor may gamble all his money on a stock he considers good, but he then exposes himself to much greater risk in the always likely event that things do not turn out as well as projected for this one company. Then too, always remember that the better you think of a company, the better others are likely to think of it, and the price may not be as undervalued as you imagine. If the stock of a company that you don't respect gives a buy signal, it is likely that others also think little of it, and the price may be too low.

The investor should decide in advance the approximate number of stocks to include in his portfolio and allot equal portions of capital to "signal" stocks as they come along. A minimum of three stocks is desirable, but there is nothing wrong with having ten, twenty, or more. After all, an aggressive investor should be watching almost all listed stocks. If possible, it is desirable to vary the amounts of money: it is better to buy only round lots in order to avoid extra commissions.

The investor interested in capital gains should always borrow as much money as possible to buy stocks. That is, he makes full use of the margin available to him from his broker for listed stocks and bank loans for unlisted stocks. Margin enables him to increase his profit expectations considerably simply because a given amount of money can buy more stock on which the potential gains far outweigh the cost of the borrowed money. True, the potential for loss increases also, but in this favorable game, gains should greatly exceed losses with the proper diversification. With margins at 50% or more, there is more than adequate protection for invested capital. Suppose an investor has $10,000 worth of stock for which he paid $5000, borrowing the other $5000. The stock exchange rule regarding margin calls is that the total worth of the account minus the amount borrowed must be greater than 25% of the total worth of the account. Thus, the investor's account would have to fall in value to $6700, a 33% drop, before he would be called on for more money. For 70% margin, the drop would have to be 60% to $4000. Such huge drops can of course occur, but the probability is small when dealing with stocks with sharply increasing earnings.

We come now to the crucial question of when to sell. And let me make one point clear right at the beginning. When playing a favorable game like the stock market in which the long-term price trend is steadily upward, you should try to remain fully invested at all times. In my opinion, nobody can forecast short-term price fluctuations, and anyone trying to play them to his advantage is more apt to miss strong price rises which usually occur at the most unexpected times. Furthermore, the chances of being "whipsawed" increase drastically, that is, you are buying when you should be selling and selling when you should be buying.

A stock should be sold *immediately* under the following two circumstances:

(1) Earnings are reported that are 10% or more below the expectations of either you, your analyst, or company officials.

(2) Either you, your analyst, or company officers downgrade the earnings estimate for a company in a given period, even if only by pennies.

The reasons should be obvious. They are the converse of those advanced for buying a stock. The company is not doing as well as expected by the market, and sooner or later, probably sooner, the market will lower the price to reflect the reduced expectations. Especially with lower-than-expected reported earnings, the drop in price is apt to be dramatic. In the second case, there may be an appreciable lag of a few days or weeks.

96

In 1967, I ignored my own principles by holding a stock after its earnings projections were downgraded by Value Line, whose estimates I was following for this particular stock. The company was the Molybdenum Corporation of America, which I had bought when the earnings projections were raised sharply late in 1966. By the following March, "Moly" had appreciated more than 50%, at which time Value Line lowered its earnings estimates very slightly. The original estimate was $4.75 per share for the 1967 calendar year, and this was reduced to $4.50 in March 1967, at which time the stock was selling for 70. I should have sold, but I had such a big profit, because I had bought in the 40 range, that I hoped to hold the stock six months to take advantage of the capital gains provision in the income tax law. Besides, the new estimate was only a bit below the previous one. Well, within a few weeks, a rash of new estimates appeared for Moly, each lower than the preceding one, and the stock plummeted to where I had originally bought it. The company ended the year with less than $2.00 per share earnings.

A more dramatic example of the effect of a changed earnings estimate on the price of a stock occurred on August 22, 1968. Sparked by a couple of big block trades, the stock of one of Wall Street's more prominent swingers, Control Data Corporation, fell over sixteen points from the close of the previous day, from an opening price of 150¼ to a closing price of 135¼. A whopping 927,000 shares were traded in all. Amid the frantic trading activity was a bevy of rumors that Control Data would report lower pro-forma earnings for the first fiscal quarter ending September 30. Some Wall Street estimates put the profit drop, including the earnings of recently merged Commercial Credit Corporation, at around the 20% level. In a telephone interview, the treasurer of the company confirmed that pro-forma earnings were likely to be down, but he declined to say to what extent. The talk in the Street was that Control Data's earnings for 1968 would run somewhere in the vicinity of 1967 results, a distinct disappointment to most analysts who had expected a better performance. The next day, the stock dropped another seven points.

Upon acquiring a stock, the investor should exercise continuous supervision over its earnings prospects. In addition to alert watching for the two sell signals described above, he should try to determine when the earnings are no longer expected to increase at a fast enough rate. A good way to do this is to keep track of The Value Line's estimated earnings for the year ending six months in the future. This figure becomes available every three months as Value Line continues its supervision of the stock. A stock should be marked for selling when this estimate fails to increase by five percent or more in successive three-month reviews. The stock was originally bought because sharply higher earnings were envisioned. Now, the less than five percent increase in earnings estimates indicates that the growth rate in earnings is slowing down, and, therefore, the price increases may vanish. Furthermore, there is little margin for error. If the forecast is slightly wrong, there could be a turndown in earnings, and you don't want to be holding a stock when this happens. The stock should be held, however, until a new buying opportunity presents itself, for any possible undervaluation remaining and also to take full advantage of the favorable stock market game. Never forget that on average all stocks go up, and one like this with a history of steadily increasing earnings should do better than average. Some investors may wish to hold this type of stock for six months, and that is permissible. If The Value Line does not review the stock, the investor must use either his own projected earnings or those of some other service.

Two reasons for not being in a hurry to sell are taxes and commissions. Profits taken from the sale of stocks held less than six months are taxed at the regular rates. For stocks held more than six months, only half the profit is taxed at the regular income tax rate up to a maximum of 25% of the total profit. In either case, the penalty to the investor is severe. I myself use two methods of softening the tax blow. First, when a market decline gives me paper losses, I am apt to sell to realize the losses no matter how promising the prospects appear for the stock. I then use the money to invest in another equally promising situation. The realized losses can be written off against past profits or carried forward for use against future profits. Second, instead of selling a stock in which I have a substantial profit when a sell signal is given, I sell it short against the box. Selling it short against the box just means that you sell short other shares of the same stock. When you do this, you still own the original shares, and in addition you have sold short the same amount of the same stock. This protects me against taking a loss in the market price: if the stock goes down, I lose money on the stock I own, but I make the same amount of money on the shares sold short. If the price should go up, I make money on the shares I own, but lose the equivalent amount on the shares sold short. Price changes in the stock no longer affect me: I still own the stock, and have not taken any profits as far as anyone else (particularly the government) is concerned. Therefore I can hold on to the stock until I wish to sell, and no taxes need be paid and no profits taken until I close out the transaction by delivering the stock I own to the lender of the shares I sold short. No money other than that for the commission on selling short need be put up. You can be short against the box indefinitely, and if you close out the short sale, no further commission is charged.

Commissions also eat into an investor's profits. Every switch of stocks costs two commissions. Since each costs about 1% of the amount of money involved, each switch deducts about 2% of your profits. The charge is less for high-priced stocks and more for low-priced stocks. I shall have more to say about taxes and commissions in the next chapter.

Do not sell for any reason other than reduced earnings prospects. Especially don't sell because of subjective feelings that the market is too high or because it looks like the bottom will drop out of the market. Many brokers play on these fears near the bottom of a long decline in the hopes of getting commissions. "Blood money" is the name for this type of business. Just remember, when you feel bluest, everybody else probably feels the same. By the time you take action to sell, everyone has sold who intended to and the market is ready for a rise. All too often, the biggest rallies begin after breathtaking sinking spells. There is probably no worse feeling for an investor than to see a stock skyrocket in price after he has sold it.

The number of buys to be expected in a year will depend on the number of stocks the investor keeps under scrutiny. I can give only a rough figure on the precise quantity, but two or three percent of the number of stocks under supervision should be about right. Thus, if an investor follows the 1400 stocks The Value Line now covers, he should find about twenty-five to fifty plays a year using the above rules. The Value Line has recently introduced quarterly estimates of earnings for the coming year, which makes it particularly easy to compare their projections with the actual reported quarterly earnings. Most other services give only yearly forecasts if they give any at all, and it is necessary for the individual investor to break them down into quarters. Such manipulation can be very time-consuming and the chances for error increase.

Once having latched on to a "signal" stock, do not let go. If it does not act well after you bought, give it a chance. Over the near term there is simply no way to predict how it will act. I remember buying Wesco Financial in 1960 because of sharply upgraded earnings estimates by Value Line at a price of 24. Soon thereafter, it had sunk to 18, but as far as I could judge, there had been no change in its excellent prospects. My patience and tenacity were well rewarded when I finally sold the stock a year later at over 50. It seems to be a common rule around Wall Street to sell a stock if it depreciates 10% or more from the initial buying price. In my opinion, such rules should be ignored. Always keep your eye on the company's prospects and forget the price fluctuations. Don't become a wigglewatcher.

In contrast, many "signal" stocks will act well from the moment of purchase. And the temptation will be strong to nail down profits after a substantial rise. After all, is a stock as "safe" after an advance to 200 as it had been at 25? Is the current price, however high, the sole measure of value? My answer to both these questions is an unqualified "yes." Don't get shaken out of a stock because the price seems too high. Never forget that other people are buying the stock at 200, and there is no reason, as long as the earnings prospects are still improving, that the stock could not go much higher. Too many investors lose the greatest part of possible capital gains by getting scared of dizzying heights. A feeling that a stock is too high in price presumes some standard of value. But I think I have shown that there is no currently accepted criterion. So, again, do not worry about the price and keep your eye fixed on the earnings prospects. Once in a while, a stock will retrace all its gain, but more often than not, truly fantastic flyers will carry you into the clouds. Hold on until a sell signal is given.

Every once in a while, you may have access to people highly placed in a company and be privy to inside information about the company and its competitors. If such information includes estimated earnings for some future period, I would use it in the manner described above. Do not use it as I did a couple of years ago. Late in 1966, the earnings projections for Control Data were upgraded sharply. Actually, while the percentage increase was enormous, the total predicted was only about 50¢

a share for 1967. With Control Data selling about 35, the price-to-earnings ratio was huge. Never let high price-to-earnings ratios scare you, however. Everybody else knows they are high as well as you do. Unfortunately, I ignored my figures until I could talk to friends of mine in both IBM and Control Data about the latter company's prospects. The opinion in both companies was the same—only slow growth was to be expected for Control Data. On the basis of this expert advice, I let the stock go. And go it went, up to a price of over 150. Trust your figures and don't listen to others unless they have a good reason for you to change them.

Following an investment program like this, you should realize at least 50% a year gain on your invested capital when the average for all stocks goes up 15% or more. If you are on margin, the 50% applies to the total worth of your account. Once in a while, a losing year will intersperse itself, but there is little you can do about it. If you try to predict the short-range behavior of the stock market, you will more than likely miss the big rises. In 1965 and 1967, I cleared well over 100% on my investments, but in 1966, I showed a slight loss. Now, I do not consider myself an aggressive investor, since most of my time is devoted to scientific research. Many is the time when surprising earnings reports appeared on the broad tape and caused a flurry of buying before I read about it in the newspapers the following day. The lost time decreases your percentage gains possibilities by quite a bit. The broad tape is the display of the up-to-the-minute business news by the Dow-Jones news service. Watching it constantly can be very rewarding, but each individual investor must decide for himself whether or not he would rather be doing something else. My experience indicates that there is usually enough of a time lag before new information is discounted to give an investor time for action.

In closing, let me summarize the buy and sell signals discussed in this chapter.

BUY SIGNALS

(1) An analyst whose earnings estimates are closely followed by the investor suddenly upgrades his forecast for a company by 10% or more, with the previous and new predictions covering the same time period;

(2) The officers themselves enlarge their company's prospective earnings by 10% or more, with the previous and new predictions covering the same period;

(3) The actual earnings reported are 10% or more greater than that forecast by the analyst or by the company officers for the period.

SELL SIGNALS

(1) Earnings are reported that are 10% or more below the expectations of either you, your analyst, or company officials;

(2) Either you, your analyst, or company officers downgrade the earnings estimate for a company in a given period;

(3) Mark a stock for selling when the earnings estimated for the year ending six months in the future fails to increase by 5% or more three months after the first estimate. Sell when a buy signal is given for another stock.

CHAPTER X

THE MANAGEMENT OF PORTFOLIOS II. CAPITAL GAINS AND INCOME FOR BEGINNERS AND DABBLERS

> To do good is noble. But to teach others to do good is more noble—and much easier.
>
> MARK TWAIN

ALL stocks are more likely to go up in price than down. And they go up to the tune of about 10% per year in appreciation plus dividends. Because of this strong upward trend, the stock market is made to order for beginners and dabblers. Pick a few stocks at random, buy them, sit back and let them appreciate in value. Nothing else need be done. Maybe they will not go up tomorrow, or next week, or next month, or even next year. But, most assuredly, over the years they will. They always have. That's why there are so many experts on the stock market. Where else can you get such an excellent return on your money and pay as much or as little attention to your investment as you please? Or have so much fun? In fact, for the inexperienced investor, paying less rather than more attention is likely to be the correct approach. Frightening fluctuations in price, rumors, tips, advice from your broker, fast-breaking news items—the pressures to buy and sell exerted by these happenings lead, in my opinion, down the most likely path to losses in the market. You are sure to be behind the market by the time you can take action, with the consequence that you will be buying stocks temporarily overpriced and selling stocks temporarily underpriced. You won't like the results, but your broker will love you.

Just buy and never sell. That's the ticket for almost certain profits in the market. Rises and declines very often come on "no news," without a warning or any dramatic development to trigger them. Anyone playing the wiggles in price is apt to miss more opportunities than not and get whipsawed in the bargain. In the November 1967 edition of *Fortune* Magazine, the buy and never sell philosophy was given a big boost. *Fortune* was examining the trading habits of the so-called performance funds, or "go-go" funds, which do heavy buying and selling of stocks. These funds have gained sizable followings on Wall Street, justifiably it seems, because they have done well in the market. But who hasn't? From what we know now of random investments, most people should do well.

Fortune did not go quite this far. But the article did suggest that the new funds' success might be quite unrelated to their heavy trading. Although they are adept at picking good stocks, "they deserve blame for frittering away their advantage by frenetic trading." *Fortune* ran tests on six funds: Fund of America, Fidelity Capital, Manhattan, Ivest, Oppenheimer, and Keystone K-2. In the first test, the funds were assumed to have held their portfolios in the last quarter of 1965 right through August 31, 1967. Of the five funds in existence during 1965—the Manhattan Fund was not—three would have done considerably better than they did by trading if they had just stood pat with the original portfolio. The other two would have done about as well as they did by trading. A similar test was then run on all six funds, this time assuming that they had kept intact the portfolios held at the end of 1966. In this test, one fund would have done far better by standing pat, two others would have done a little better by standing pat, and the other three did a little better by trading. For a final test, *Fortune* contrasted the performance of stock bought by five of the funds in the fourth quarter of 1966 (the sixth fund, Keystone K-2, was omitted because it did not report for that quarter) with the subsequent performance of stock sold by the same funds in that quarter. Stock sold by two of the five funds did far better than stock bought. Stock sold did a little better than stock bought for another fund, and about equally well for still another. For only one fund, Ivest, did stock bought significantly outperform stock sold.

The funds usually buy into companies whose earnings prospects look good. Here they are on firm ground. Why they sell is difficult to say. If they have a large turnover in a single quarter, sometimes it seems as though they have not given their stocks a chance to appreciate. In Chapter VII we learned that it takes upwards of a year for a stock with sharply improved earnings prospects to discount the new information. What is of most interest in this inquiry to the beginner and dabbler, however, is the recognition that buying and holding is proven to be a sound policy.

If you are a beginner or dabbler, how do you go about picking stocks for a portfolio so that you can expect to do as well as anybody else, or maybe even better? Three ways suggest themselves:

(1) Pick a mutual fund, put your money into it, and forget it;

(2) Decide how many stocks you would like to have in your portfolio, divide your money into that many portions, and then pick the appropriate number of stocks blindly;

(3) Do a little work to find out about earnings estimates and buy only those stocks with sharply increasing earnings prospects.

The first way isn't much fun, but many people seem to prefer it. The tricky part of the second method is to select stocks at random, or blindly. It is not as easy as it sounds. So preposterous does this idea of random selection appear that very few people will really act on it. They will look and listen here, there, and everywhere for advice and opinion from people who supposedly know more than they. Or they will study all the literature they can find on a stock of interest so as to convince themselves of the company's merit. Both courses would lead to mistakes in the sense that stocks would be bought the qualities of which are well-known and adequately discounted in the market place. They are apt to do more poorly than they should. Never, never forget you are playing against all other investors, and we have seen the excellence of their collective judgment. Don't make the error of thinking you know more than anybody else unless there is good reason to think so.

I knew somebody who would go through an amazingly exhaustive and detailed analysis of any company in which he took an interest for investment purposes. He would study the industry or industries the company was part of, read descriptive material on the company, dissect its financial statements, examine recent prospectuses, and even telephone the company president to clear up any vague points. After digesting all the information and satisfying himself as to the company's worth, he would invest his money. His record of profit and loss was completely incomprehensible to him. Regularly, the stocks he bought declined after purchase, and only after a long holding period of two or three years would the stock get back to where he had bought it. When I suggested that he emphasize changes in projected earnings in his analyses, he was quite surprised.

It had never occurred to him that guesses about the future could be important, that anything but cold, hard facts should be considered. But he was quick to understand that the cold, hard facts he paid attention to were ancient history as far as stock prices were concerned, and he is now making up for past errors.

You might use Senator McIntyre's technique of dart throwing for random selection. Or you might have your children pick out stocks they like, in which case, you can boast to your friends how you profited on your kid's stocks. Many other ways can be dreamed up. But, most importantly, don't listen to any advice. Or, if you do, buy only those stocks which are not liked or on which the comment is non-committal. If you want dividend income, buy only those stocks yielding the desired amount. If you want capital gains and are not worried about current income, buy only those stocks with low or no yields. Overall, considering appreciation and dividend yield, you will probably do equally well no matter which type of stock comprises your portfolio. According to Lorie and Fisher, about 10% per year, although the rate seems to have increased to about 15% since 1950. Such a performance would equal and probably surpass most mutual funds, especially those funds which charge premiums to buy into them. This premium is called a loading charge, and it can run upwards of 10% on your investment.

Now, what about the beginner or dabbler who wishes to do better than average? Is there an investment program for him that will not use up all his time, a program that will demand, say, only a few hours a week? There is, and the amount of time put in will depend on just how many stocks he wishes to follow. First, it is necessary to subscribe to some service that keeps stocks, the more the better, under constant supervision. This means, essentially, that earnings projections are made regularly. Second, when an earnings estimate is made, note the amount and the time period for which it applies. Third, when the stock is next reviewed, again note the earnings estimate and the time period. Fourth, calculate the percentage change in the earnings estimate if the two estimates are for the same time period. Fifth, purchase the stock if the new earnings estimate is 10% or more higher than the old estimate.

An example will help illuminate the details. On March 8, 1968, The Value Line Investment Survey estimated the earnings of Homestake Mining Company at $1.60 per share for the calendar year 1968. On June 7, 1968, this estimate for calendar 1968 was raised to $2.10 per share. The change in the earnings per share amounted to an increase of 50¢ per share. If the latter figure is now divided by the original estimate, $1.60, and the result multiplied by 100, we obtain the percentage increase. Thus, .50 divided by 1.60 equals .31, and multiplying by 100 gives 31%. According to the above rules, Homestake Mining should be bought. Something was happening during the time period between the two estimates that caused the analyst to raise his projections for Homestake sharply. In this case, the reason was clear. Gold, Homestake's major product, was going up in price.

The number of stocks an investor wishes to hold in his portfolio is up to him. I would recommend that at least three be bought. Divide the money earmarked for investment into approximately equal portions, as many as the number of stocks desired. When a buying opportunity comes along, use one portion of the money to buy the stock. Continue the process until all money is committed.

When do you sell? Never, if you prefer. As you gather in cash, just accumulate stocks and sit with them. For upwards of a year after purchase, the stocks bought will do better than average. After that time, you can expect average performance. As new stocks that have given buy signals are added to your portfolio, you can expect better than average performance.

For those beginners and dabblers who wish to continue to do better than average, proceed as follows. Mark a stock for selling when the change in the earnings estimate is less than 5% higher than the previous estimate. Then, when a new stock comes along that gives a buy signal, sell and purchase the new stock.

People often ask me when the best time is to get into the stock market, and my answer is any time you have the available cash. I do not believe anyone can foresee the short-term fluctuations in stock prices, despite the fact that much ado is made of a whole array of mystical indicators. Some of these are the advance-decline lines, the odd-lot indices, short interest ratio, odd-lot short selling. There are many others. Sometimes these work and sometimes they do not, like the magic of witch doctors. Very often, they contradict one another or fail to give clear signals. If you have sold because of one of these technical indicators, which has now reversed itself, you are left out in the cold wondering whether or not to buy back in. You will never be sure when to buy, and while you hesitate the market is likely to go up. One of the worst aspects of selling on technical signals is that bottoms are rarely pinpointed and you miss the big advances.

All I can say is that I know that the market will go up. When it will do so, however, cannot be specified. In the fall of 1967, one of my friends had a large sum of money to invest. The time hardly seemed propitious according to the technical indicators, most of which suggested that the market was in for a period of weakness. On my advice, my friend ignored them and purchased stocks whose earnings projections were rising. These stocks did well through the market weakness of early 1968, and at this writing in late spring have scored substantial profits. Keep in mind the fact that the stock market acts like a bouncing ball, only in reverse. With a ball, the bounces become smaller and smaller and the ball eventually settles on the ground. But with the market, the bounces become larger and larger and prices always keep going up. Do not let the short-term fluctuations obscure the strong upward trend.

Suppose we look at the results we could have had if we bought the stocks whose earnings prospects were raised 10% or more by The Value Line in the period July 23, 1965 to October 15, 1965 and we held them all through June 1968. The earnings prospects refer to the year ending six months in the future, but similar results would have been obtained if the next fiscal year were used. Two hundred twelve stocks gave signals—estimates of earnings increases—and their average appreciation was 91%. By contrast, the average appreciation of Value Line's 1100 stocks was 55% over this period. If only those stocks whose earnings projections were raised by 20% or more were bought, the average increase in price was 109%, or more than double the initial cost. This difference between 91% and 109% is statistically significant, so an investor may wish to buy only those stocks with increases in earnings projections greater than 20%. To these average appreciation figures dividends must be added. Dividends amounted to about 8% over that period. And, of course, about 1% must be substracted for brokerage commissions.

A look at the distribution of percentage gains proves interesting. Of the two hundred twelve stocks giving the 10% buy signal, twenty-one showed a loss over the period, sixty-nine showed gains ranging from 0% to 49%, thirty-seven from 50% to 99%, fifty-seven from 100% to 199%, sixteen from 200% to 299%, and twelve grew in value by 300% or more. One hundred twenty-two of these stocks gained 50% or more, so our investor had better than a fifty-fifty chance of scoring a capital gain greater than 50% on his money over this period. Eighty-five stocks more than doubled in price, which meant there was a 40% chance of doubling the original investment. On the other side of the coin, twenty-one stocks showed a decline in price, giving a 10% chance of a loss.

There is little doubt that a roaring bull market existed during this time period, a bull market that perhaps will not be repeated for a while. Certainly the rate of gain is far above the 10% measured by Fisher and Lorie: about double, in fact. However, we are interested in comparative performance, and it was those stocks with sharp jumps in earnings prospects that definitely performed best.

Now what about the more aggressive beginner or dabbler who keeps his portfolio under constant supervision, trying always to have the best possible stocks? He will purchase those stocks for which earnings estimates are increased 10% or more. The time period for the two estimates should be the same. Alternatively, if The Value Line is used for earnings estimates, the estimates for the year ending six months in the future can be used. Suppose our beginner or dabbler decides he wants ten stocks in his portfolio. He divides his money into ten equal parts and buys those stocks giving signals until he is fully committed. As long as the earnings estimate for a stock is raised 5% or more at each review, he holds on to it. If the earnings estimate for a stock does not increase by at least 5%, he marks it for sale and sells when a new buying opportunity for another stock comes along, using the money to buy the new stock. What results can be expected?

We cover the same period as before, 1965 to 1968. Ten stocks for which The Value Line raised its earnings projections 10% or more in the period July 23, 1965 to October 15, 1965 are initially bought at random from the two hundred twelve stocks giving signals. At every three-month review by The Value Line, the new earnings projection for the year ending six months in the future is noted, and if this figure is 5% or more above the one from the previous review, the stock is held. Otherwise, it is sold and a new stock giving a signal is

112

bought. Doing this for many ten-stock portfolios selected at random from those stocks giving signals yields an expected appreciation of 146% on the initial investment, considering the time period through June 1968. Counting dividends, this is over 50% per year. However, there is a small catch in this method because of commissions and taxes. Let us go over a sample ten-stock portfolio that an investor may have bought in July 1965. In the July 23, 1965 issue of The Value Line Investment Survey, the earnings projections of twenty-two stocks for the year ending six months in the future were raised 10% or more from the previous review three months earlier. The first ten in my records at the time are: American Bosch at 20, Bendix at 50, Rohr at 25, Thiokol at 14, Ford at 52, General Motors at 96, Gulf and Western at 38, Hoover Ball Bearings at 31, Eltra at 34, and Budd at 16. We assume that our investor puts an equal amount of money into each of these ten stocks. The subsequent changes in earnings estimates and price for each of these stocks are then noted. Three months later on October 22, 1965, the percentage appreciation for each stock is shown in the following list:

American Bosch	20%
Bendix	24%
Rohr	36%
Thiokol	36%
Ford	15%
General Motors	13%
Gulf & Western	100%
Hoover Ball	45%
Eltra	12%
Budd	25%

Also on October 22, 1965, Value Line's earnings projections for the year ending six months in the future increased less than 5% compared to the projection three months earlier for American Bosch, Rohr, Thiokol, Ford, General Motors, and Hoover Ball Bearings. These stocks were sold and replaced

113

with new stocks which gave signals on October 22. The new list of stocks, together with their price appreciation in the three months ending January 21, 1966 follows:

Beech Aircraft	35%
Bendix	10%
Boeing	40%
Cessna Aircraft	24%
Fairchild Hiller	43%
General Dynamics	23%
Gulf & Western	29%
Grumman	36%
Eltra	26%
Budd	5%

Beech Aircraft replaced American Bosch, Boeing replaced Rohr, Cessna replaced Thiokol, Fairchild replaced Ford, General Dynamics replaced General Motors, Grumman replaced Hoover Ball Bearings in our portfolio, a total of twelve commissions being paid for buying and selling. All the original money put into American Bosch plus the 20% made on its three-month appreciation was put into Beech Aircraft, and the same was done for each of the other changes. On January 21, 1966, only Grumman was eliminated from the portfolio and replaced by Aerojet-General. The new list with price appreciation for the three-month period ending April 22, 1966 follows:

Beech Aircraft	9%
Bendix	18%
Boeing	25%
Cessna Aircraft	10%
Fairchild Hiller	0%
General Dynamics	12%
Gulf & Western	21%
Aerojet-General	−6%
Eltra	0%
Budd	−14%

New stocks to replace the old are chosen in order of appearance in my records, of course with the qualification that they show at least a 10% increase in the earnings projection. On April 22, Aerojet-General, Boeing, Fairchild Hiller, General Dynamics, and Budd were sold, to be replaced by Douglas, Grumman, Ling-Temco-Vought, Martin Marietta, and Northrop. The new list with appreciations in price in the three months ending July 22, 1966 follows:

Beech Aircraft	−8%
Bendix	−9%
Douglas	−38%
Cessna Aircraft	−11%
Grumman	−20%
Ling-Temco-Vought	−9%
Gulf & Western	−18%
Martin Marietta	4%
Eltra	8%
Northrop	−13%

We can stop here and see what we have. The original investment in American Bosch, which represents one-tenth of our capital, grew 20% in the first three months. Suppose a thousand dollars had been invested in each of the ten stocks. That thousand dollars in American Bosch appreciated 20% at the end of three months. The gain in dollars is figured by multiplying $1000 by 20% or 0.20.

$$
\begin{array}{r}
\$1000 \\
\times \ .20 \\
\hline
\$ \ 200
\end{array}
$$

Therefore, after three months, the original $1000 was worth $1200.

The $1200 was then invested in Beech Aircraft, which then appreciated 35% in the following three months. In dollars, the gain is $420.

$$
\begin{array}{r}
\$1200 \\
\times \ .35 \\
\hline
\$ \ 420
\end{array}
$$

Our original $1000 is now worth $1620.

115

Beech Aircraft was held for the next three months as well and appreciated a further 9%. The gain on $1620 is $145.80, so our original $1000 is now worth $1765.80.

$$\begin{array}{r} \$1620 \\ \times \ .09 \\ \hline \$ \ 145.80 \end{array}$$

In the next three months, Beech was still held and declined 8%. This represents a loss of $141.26 on $1765.80.

$$\begin{array}{r} \$1765.80 \\ \times \ \ \ \ .08 \\ \hline \$ \ 141.26 \end{array}$$

We now have a total capital of $1624.54.

If this process is continued through June 1968, our original $1000 in American Bosch would end up as $1690, a gain of 69% on our investment. Every original dollar is worth $1.69. The record is shown in Table II beginning with the row on which AB (the stock exchange symbol for American Bosch) appears. The numbers in each column are the percentage appreciations of stocks in the three months following the dates at the head of each column. All the original stocks bought on July 23, 1965 appear in the left hand column. New stocks appear in each row on the date they give a buy signal, followed by the percentage gain in the next three months. Where no stock symbol appears in a column, the first stock to the left in that row was held. The right hand column gives the final compounded percent gain for the series of stocks in each row. Stocks in the first row, as already indicated, yielded a gain of 69% on the original investment. Stocks in the second row, beginning with BX (Bendix) yielded a 139% gain. If $1000 was originally put into Bendix and the indicated transactions were carried out, the gain was $1390.

$$\begin{array}{r} \$1000 \\ \times\ 1.39 \\ \hline \$1390 \end{array}$$

The initial $1000 therefore became $2390. For any arbitrary initial investment, the gain in dollars is found by just multiplying the compounded percent gain by the original investment.

Similarly, for the third row, the compounded percent gain was 90%, so every initial dollar invested in RHR (Rohr Corporation) was worth $1.90.

If the compounded percent gains are averaged for the ten rows of stocks, the result is 157%. This means that for this particular portfolio, every dollar originally invested in the ten stocks shown in the left hand column of Table II was in the end worth more than 2½ times as much, or $2.57, a profit of $1.57 on each original dollar.

If the same procedure is followed for many different portfolios, randomly selecting those stocks giving signals, the expectation is that a gain of 146% on the original investment would have been made over this time period. This compares to the 91% for those investors buying on signals and never selling and 55% for the comprehensive Value Line stock average. It is extremely unlikely that anyone could approach these results by random selection from all stocks listed on the stock exchanges. Therefore, the system is a valid one.

The small catch in this method of portfolio management lies in the commissions and income taxes. A full 10% of the gain gets eaten up by commissions.

In addition to the commission bite, there is the income tax. Any of the short-term gains realized on this ten-stock portfolio are taxed as regular income, while long-term gains are taxed at the capital gains rate. It is likely that at least 25% of the profits will go for taxes, and 10% for commissions, bringing the average three-year gain down to about 110%, almost

TABLE II. Performance of a sample ten-stock portfolio managed in accordance with the principles developed in Chapter X over the period July 1965 to July 1968. The dates at the head of each column designate three-month intervals. When a stock symbol appears under a given date, a buy signal for that stock was given on that date. When this

7/23/65	10/22/65	1/21/66	4/22/66	7/22/66	10/21/66	1/20/67
AB 20%	BCX 35%	9%	−8%	−23%	NOC 33%	GQ −18%
BX 24	10	18	−9	MAC −31	45	HH 14
RHR 36	BA 40	25	D −38	FRC −10	50	GWD −13
THI 36	CEA 24	10	−11	−30	THI 42	35
F 15	FEN 43	0	GQ −20	KW 0	4	GLB 3
GM 13	GD 23	12	LTV −9	−31	116	33
GW 100	29	21	−18	−31	68	30
HBB 45	GQ 36	AJT −6	ML 4	−25	MRQ 25	−7
ET 12	26	0	8	−25	GUL 49	53
BF 25	5	−14	NOC −13	MAR −22	22	DAY 4

the same as for the investor who buys on signals and never sells. Some relief from the tax situation can be obtained by the two methods described in the last chapter. But each individual investor must determine for himself how best to meet the tax payments.

If we limit our portfolio selections to those stocks that not only show a 10% or more increase in earnings projections, but also did not decline in price in the three months prior to the new projection, the Group Aa stocks of Chapter VII, the expected appreciation goes up to 192%, significantly higher than the 146% just obtained.

In order to reduce commissions and taxes, we will consider a stock is marked for selling only when the earnings estimate for it is less than the preceding estimate. Previously, we marked a stock for selling when the earnings estimate for the year ending six months in the future failed to increase by 5% or more in successive three-month reviews. In all other rehappens, the stock whose symbol appears to the left of that column is sold and the proceeds invested in the new stock as of the date at the head of the column. The numbers represent the percentage change in price in the three-month period beginning with the date at the head of the column for the stock whose symbol is to the left.

4/21/67	7/21/67	10/20/67	1/19/68	4/19/68	Compounded percent gain
CW 14%	BA −20%	RHR 33%	−11%	CEA 15%	69%
GD 44	UA −19	C 12	17	−6	139%
ET 15	AMO 0	HBB −9	AJT −7	14	90%
MCR 10	4	0	CW −8	FEN −8	116%
EAL 10	BF 18	BOR 14	MD −2	17	139%
34	10	CHM 8	GM 5	GQ 9	414%
27	GWD 1	LOF −2	MFG −14	ML 9	355%
8	GBY −10	EAL −9	SMC 0	PPA 19	75%
41	−5	−18	GWD −21	AMO 8	208%
TWA −24	AAE 18	NAL −18	GY −10	7	−33%
				Average	157%

spects, the rules for buying and selling will remain the same. This change in our sell signal results in fewer changes in the portfolio and, therefore, in longer holding periods for the stocks.

Using this method, the average appreciation of twenty-five ten-stock portfolios selected at random over the period from 1965 through June 1968 was 127%, compared to 146% under the previous rules. Although the appreciation is now significantly less, now only 6% is taken off for commissions, compared to 10% previously. Furthermore, many more stocks are held for time periods of six months or longer so that advantage of the smaller capital gains tax can be taken. All in all, there does not seem to be any advantage of one method over the other when appreciation, commissions, and taxes are considered. A sample portfolio is shown in Table III.

A significant improvement in results occurs when only those stocks are bought that show a 20% or more increase in their

TABLE III. Performance of a sample ten-stock portfolio managed in accordance with the principles developed in Chapter X over the period August 1965 to July 1968. The only dif-

8/27/65	11/26/65	2/25/66	5/26/66	8/26/66	11/25/66
COG 52%	68%	−24%	APC −25%	−12%	OXP 10%
CR 24	49	−19	−17	3	WRN 2
FJQ −5	DSO 4	−13	−5	−20	BDC 48
RHE 14	16	−21	GLW 16	−13	20
WW 4	KI 56	−29	−14	−5	48
WAB 5	30	4	EPI −3	−4	22
WY −7	3	−7	−11	WW −14	BKR 50
H * 4	15	−6	−10	−12	26
HML 11	MNC 5	−20	EVY −8	−47	CRI 29
SRT 0	18	−18	−6	−10	FPC 40

earnings projections. This figure is double the 10% increase used previously. If the previous estimate for the year ending six months in the future was $1.00 per share, the new figure would have to be $1.20 or more for a buy signal to be given. A stock is marked for selling when the new estimate fails to increase by 5% or more. With these rules, the average increase in initial capital over many ten-stock portfolios is 205%, three times the original amount invested. Fewer stocks give 20% buy signals, and if this procedure is followed, the investor may have to exercise some patience until one comes along. Table IV shows the performance of a sample portfolio covering the same data in my records as Table III. Note the improvement.

One final point. Don't miss buying a stock because of an eighth or a quarter of a point. When a buy comes along, buy at the market. When a sell comes along, sell at the market. Nothing hurts as much as when a stock doubles, only you missed it by having an order to buy an eighth of a point below the market.

ference in procedure from Table II is that stocks are marked for selling only when the earnings estimate declines from that made three months previously.

2/24/67	5/25/67	8/25/67	11/24/67	2/23/68	Compounded percent gain
APC 9%	0%	AAC 17%	14%	25%	156%
AMZ 12	−7	AST −7	31	9	80%
−8	EVY 13	−23	0	4	−20%
4	−4	JWC 2	17	24	87%
0	33	6	24	0	143%
FJQ 19	79	3	17	51	525%
22	9	8	15	0	69%
BWN 10	MQC 0	DXC −12	0	AMZ 13	23%
27	4	RII 6	12	32	21%
−5	20	WBL 13	CRT 6	59	149%
					Average 123%

* H is Hudson Pulp and Paper, an over-the-counter stock.

In summary, the beginner and dabbler has three courses open to him if he decides to invest in common stocks. These are as follows:

(1) He can put his money into a mutual fund and forget it;

(2) He can decide how many stocks he wants in his portfolio, divide his money into that many portions, and then select the appropriate number of stocks blindly;

(3) He can do a little work to find out about earnings estimates and invest only in those stocks for which the estimates are increased 10% or more from the previous review of the same advisory service.

Once owning the stocks, the investor need never sell. Those investors choosing procedure (3) will do better than average even if they never sell. They will do even better if they mark a stock for sale when the earnings projection fails to increase by 5% and sell when a buy comes along, putting the money into the new stock. Or alternatively, they can mark a stock for

TABLE IV. Performance of a sample ten-stock portfolio managed in accordance with the principles developed in Chapter X over the period August 1965 to July 1968. Buy signals for stocks occur when the earnings estimate for the year

8/27/65	11/26/65	2/25/66	5/26/66	8/26/66	11/25/66
COG 52%	68%	−24%	APC −25%	−12%	BKR 50%
WW 4	KI 56	−29	−14	−5	48
H * 4	MNC 5	FO −22	CR −17	3	SHK 83
BDC 61	16	0	4	−7	48
BKR 17	13	WMC −6	−6	−20	LFE 32
FCI 80	58	−26	23	−47	SK 71
HVE 13	28	NH −24	EPI −3	WW −14	WEC 35
HEC 103	60	−30	RII −10	PUL −14	CDA 73
ITE 35	BWN 62	5	−14	AVT −6	44
SGM 63	−10	11	−6	−14	CF 42

selling if the earnings projection declines from the previous review by the same service and sell when a buy comes along, putting the money into the new stock. Over the period 1965 to 1968, when the average price of all stocks went up by 55%, those investors who bought signal stocks (those with increases of 10% or more in projected earnings) and never sold had an ending six months in the future increases by 20% or more. A stock is marked for selling when the estimate fails to increase by 5% or more, and it is sold when a buy is signaled for another stock.

2/24/67	5/25/67	8/25/67	11/24/67	2/23/68	Compounded percent gain
FJQ 19%	79%	3%	17%	51%	646%
0	DXC 44	−12	0	KCG 47	159
WBL −6	PUL 4	−5	CRT 6	59	109
HEC 0	AV 12	−16	INP 26	10	249
DES 7	BKR 9	AST −7	KI 24	0	66
HSC 37	SK −3	EVY −23	LPT 0	UPC 38	231
SSH −13	APY 0	JWC 2	17	24	59
81	24	30	MQC 0	WBL 56	1285
52	3	70	−19	51	770
AZ 26	TDY 12	32	NH 42	122	999
					Average 457%

* H is Hudson Pulp and Paper.

average gain of 91%. Those who sold on the 5% sell signal had an average gain of 146%, and those who sold on declining earnings estimates had an average gain of 127%.

Those investors waiting for a 20% increase in earnings estimates to buy would have tripled their money over this period.

CHAPTER XI

THE OVER-THE-COUNTER MARKET

Full many a flower is born to blush unseen,
And waste its sweetness on the desert air.

THOMAS GRAY, *Elegy Written in a
Country Churchyard*

LIKE an iceberg, its real substance largely hidden from view, the over-the-counter market is an unknown quantity to the public and even to a fair proportion of professionals. There is no ticker tape to cover the flow and nature of trading, no volume figures are published in the daily newspapers, and it is only recently that the public has been able to find meaningful quotations in the papers. The trading rooms—where shirt-sleeved traders, with their peculiar air of being absolutely alone in a crowded room, sit behind banks of telephones in a welter of flashing lights, half-eaten sandwiches, piled up directories, crumpled papers, and risk millions of dollars to an anvil chorus of ringing telephones and shouted fragments of names and numbers—are seldom visited by the public. Anonymity prevails. Even on the telephones, trades are made in a dispassionate exchange of clipped, highly stylized phrases and markets—bid, offer, counter-bid, counter-offer, and so on.

The number of issues traded is huge. All government securities are traded here. Anomalously, while all United States Treasury Bonds and most publicly-owned corporates are listed on one of the exchanges, virtually all trading is conducted in the off-board, over-the-counter markets, and it is an occasion for astonishment when a trade in "Treasurys" is made on the stock exchange. Preferred stocks, too, are traded over-the-counter, in the main; the stock exchanges even maintain an "exempt list" of those in which off-floor (unlisted) dealings can be made.

The unlisted market is host to a huge body of common stocks. Virtually all bank and insurance stocks, many old and respected industrial and utility issues, most foreign shares are traded here. And of course, there is the great body of low-grade shares, too spindly in terms of investment substance to qualify for listing on an exchange. They are known as "cats and dogs." Finally, most hybrid issues—and this includes warrants, participating certificates, depositary receipts, real estate investment trusts, certificates of beneficial interest, business trusts, royalty interests, and in a very limited way, mutual fund shares—are traded over-the-counter.

The rise of the "Third Market," in which blocks of listed stocks are traded directly between institutions, or else through the services of a broker who is not a member of an exchange, and traded at cut-rate commissions, is a recent development. It serves to enlarge the volume of the off-board market at the expense of the various stock exchanges.

In terms of sheer numbers of issues traded, the unlisted over-the-counter markets far outweigh the exchanges. During a ten-month period in 1961-1962, the Securities and Exchange Commission found that broker-dealers advertised markets in 14,000 domestic over-the-counter stocks and in 3340 United States, other government, and corporate bond issues. At that same time, only 3041 stock and 1284 bond issues were listed on all domestic stock exchanges. It is true that many of the unlisted issues are narrowly or only infrequently traded, so the volume disparity is not nearly as wide as it first appears. But the large size of bank and institutional transactions in bonds and debt evidences of varying types, when added to the stock totals, pushes the unlisted dollar turnover far ahead of that generated on the stock exchanges.

The over-the-counter market is a vast, fertile ground for speculative and venture capital. Research information and company statistics are usually sketchy, and many companies that are traded were born in the very recent past. There is a steady life cycle in progress in the population of over-the-counter, unlisted, corporations. The birth of a public corporation—its initial underwriting or public sale—takes place in the over-the-counter market. As the young company grows, its securities undergo a seasoning process, in which the block holdings of insiders and large owners are gradually, day by day, lot by lot, shifted to a much larger body of stockholders. The creation of a substantial body of stockholders produces a buffering effect on price swings in the market. A flow of bite-sized bids and offers makes for a smooth market, as opposed to the abrupt moves imposed on a market by the offering of a large block of stock for sale, with no interested buyers of any magnitude present.

In general, the unlisted market offers more appealing opportunities for profit to investors with patience than it offers to fast traders. Markets here often lack the depth of those found on the stock exchanges—although the smaller size of many of the unlisted companies really makes it an unfair comparison—and it is difficult for the trader in the securities of a smaller corporation to acquire or dispose of a substantial number quickly. Shares of some large unlisted corporations, on the other hand, such as American Express, Eli Lilly, or First National City Bank, to name only a few, enjoy broad markets because of the number of top-grade investment banking houses willing to position the shares, that is, hold a large block of shares, but these cases are in the minority. In any event, thin markets are a hazard to be contemplated beforehand, rather than complained of later.

An investment in a young and aggressive corporation will usually afford the investor a better chance to increase his capital than a similar investment in securities of a large and mature corporation. It is obviously easier for a company to increase earnings from one million to two million dollars than from one billion to two billion dollars. New companies, embodying radically new processes, products, or technologies, are found in the unlisted markets in relative abundance, and the astute purchaser of these securities can often profit handsomely. Polaroid and Xerox shares dwelled in the over-the-counter market for a long time before they became listed. Hand in hand with enlarged potential for gain in these smaller firms, though, goes increased risk of loss, and prospecting off the beaten path can be dangerous in the extreme. The probability of ruin is high.

Quite apart from the high-risk, high-growth stocks, there may be better values among issues in the over-the-counter market than in comparable stocks traded on an exchange. Because public attention is focused on listed issues, these tend to sell at higher price-to-earnings multiples than do comparable unlisted equities. Accordingly, more growth, more earnings capacity, and more dividends, in terms of dollars being put to work by investors, may be found among good quality OTC stocks. Very commonly, the prospective listing on an exchange of an unlisted stock causes a sharp rise in its price as a result of widening public interest.

The term "over-the-counter" was coined over a century ago to describe the way stocks of smaller, less well-known companies were traded. In the early years of our capital markets, in order to conclude a purchase or sale of a stock issue not dealt in on one of the exchanges, customers literally made the rounds of offices of the brokers known to be "close" to a given security. When the best bid or offer had been found, a bargain was struck across the office counter of the firm. The first government certificates to finance the War of Independence were traded OTC in 1776, at a time when Philadelphia was the financial center of America. In the days when England ruled the seas, and sailing ships were king, shares in ship cargoes were traded in a special section of the bank floor designated as the "counter," giving rise to the designation "over-the-counter," to describe a market for securities in England.

Today, despite the passage of many years and the development of rapid communications media, and the creation of a vast new fund of investor knowledge and information, the basic techniques of transacting business over-the-counter differ only in scale from those of bygone eras. But because the use of telephones has rendered unnecessary the physical presence of the opposite party to a transaction, the term "over-the-counter" is no longer truly descriptive. The over-the-counter market has so many variations of form, function, location, and participants as to defy real description. It is a large, amorphous, nation-wide, local, non-focused but non-diffused market, in which the best and the worst categories of security quality are found. Shares of the smallest and largest companies are traded here, by numerous firms ranging from long established and heavily capitalized investment houses to a few "boiler room" operations that are here today and will be gone tomorrow. Because of the relative obscurity of the over-the-counter market and the opportunities it offers for large capital gain, I shall devote a few pages to describing its form and functions.

From a broad view, the over-the-counter market performs a twofold function: (1) through the sale of new offerings to investors, capital is provided for the public and private portions of our economy; and (2) in the form of registered secondary offerings, as well as in the day-to-day wholesale-retail train of activities, liquidity is afforded to security owners. Looked at conversely, the market provides would-be owners with the means of acquiring their securities.

The essence of OTC dealings is said to be "negotiation" rather than "auction" which prevails on the stock exchanges. Le Corbusier's famous maxim that form follows function is as true in finance as in architecture. The ebb and flow of security prices on the stock exchanges, visible every day on the stock tickers and financial pages of the nation, are produced in the swirl of a continuous auction market. Basic to this market is a large number of informed buyers and sellers. The collective interaction of their opinions determines the level of equilibrium of security prices, and in the tradition of Adam Smith, any overweighing of either side makes immediate impact in the form of a sharp change in prices to find a new level at which supply and demand will balance.

On the stock exchanges, a single auction market exists for each stock. This market is run by a person known as the "specialist" for the issue. The specialist collects all orders to buy and sell and enters them into a book together with the designated prices, if any. Suppose you wish to buy 100 shares of American Telephone at $51 a share. You tell your broker what you want and he communicates the information to his firm's representative on the floor of the stock exchange, the floor broker. The floor broker goes to where the specialist in Telephone holds forth and gives him the order. If some other person has offered to sell 100 shares of Telephone at $51 a share, the transaction is consummated. If not, your order is entered on the specialist's book until the proper offering comes along. There is no negotiation of price. Similarly, if you want to sell 100 shares of Telephone at $51 a share, you must wait until someone will buy at that price. When buying or selling a stock, you can ask your broker for the bid and asked prices. He will then obtain from the specialist the highest bid price for 100 shares of the stock and the lowest offering price for 100 shares. You can then decide whether or not to buy at the offered price or sell at the bid price, or whether you want to put an order on the book at your own price. We shall see that matters work differently in the over-the-counter market, where negotiation prevails.

The reaction of the classical auction market to a dominance of selling pressure is a price drop. This usually brings demand up to the level of supply, and creates a new equilibrium. When corporations raise new capital by selling a large issue of stock, or a large owner seeks to liquidate all or some of his holdings in a corporation, the result is the same—the creation of a large new supply of stock to be sold, for which buyers must be found preferably without upsetting the market price of the stock, either on the stock exchange or in the unlisted market. To handle this situation, over the years investment bankers have gradually erected an extensive and highly workable set of procedures for moving blocks of securities speedily, and the home of these efforts is in the over-the-counter markets. I shall not go into the investment banking and underwriting functions in detail, but in concept (as distinct from practice) the business is simple. The underwriting firms purchase the security from the stock issuer at a discount off the current price, and then they parcel it out, selling small amounts to their horde of small investor customers. This cushions and diffuses any impact on price. The investment firms retain a portion of the discount as their compensation in the process.

The important difference, which places the transaction in a category apart, is the purchase of the block by the bankers at a discount from the prevailing price on the exchange. In an auction market like the stock exchange, every transaction is public, and the price received on the sale of 100 shares of

130

stock becomes the ruling price for every one of the other out-standing shares. For a single moment, or at least until the next sale, the buyer and seller of that round lot have left their mark on the world of finance. The tyranny of the tape imposes this price on ten thousand or a hundred thousand other stockholders who were not involved in this transaction. But, as one of Wall Street's larger traders recently put it, "size trades at its own level." Most large block trades are more efficiently handled off-board, with no tape to hamper traders, or tell the world that a block has been traded and is in the process of distribution.

In the over-the-counter market, there is no one single public market, only a collection of individual bids and offers which may be identical or different and which are made by dealers interested in the security. A sale of stock to one dealer has no effect on any of the other markets, unless that dealer adjusts his inventory by selling some of that stock to his competitors. Transactions are negotiated in the strictest privacy and it is considered a breach of traders' etiquette to disclose to another dealer the details of a trade.

Each dealer market-maker goes his independent way, caring about other markets than his own only as a reference point. He bids and offers higher or lower, and buys and sells to add to or decrease his inventory, all in accordance with his opinion of the short-term price direction of the stock he trades. This is a negotiated market to the extent that the trader adjusts his quotations to the kind of quarry he wants to trap—a buyer or a seller. The greater part of all transactions take place on a dealer's bid or offer, and haggling, or negotiating for a better price, is relatively rare since the order broker runs the risk of "losing his market" by bargaining. After the dealer sets a market price, any counter bid or counter offer by the order broker immediately releases the dealer from the obligation of honoring the first price, on which the broker is trying to improve.

There is much that is awkward in the unlisted markets. A great deal of the clumsiness involved in getting markets and filling orders has to do with the diffused, non-centralized character of the market. The necessity of "shopping around" to find the best bid and lowest offer (the "inside market") among several dealers in a stock, some of whom may be in another city or have nothing substantial in hand at the moment, is a great time-waster compared to the ease with which prices can be checked and orders executed at a single trading post on the exchanges. Security prices change in sudden jumps—traders say a stock is "running" when this happens —and not in a gradual trend from the old price plateau to a new one. In some extreme cases, by the time a broker has checked several dealers and consumed only a few seconds of time doing it, the price of the stock he wants to buy may have moved up or down substantially, and away from his limit. In physics, the uncertainty principle declares that the process of observing a phenomenon alters it. When several brokers have checked a market in quick succession, the dealer is alerted to the possible presence of a buyer or seller, and a shrewd dealer may anticipate an order by changing his price for that stock violently before the broker has even had a chance to fill his order. This is not considered bad form, incidentally, provided the broker with the order has not disclosed to this dealer what it is he wants to do. On the other hand, it would be a serious breach of trading ethics for the dealer to "run ahead" of the broker at any point after he had been informed by the broker of his order.

In most dealings in listed securities, members of the various exchanges act as brokers for their customers for a standard commission rate and assume none of the financial risks of ownership in bringing the securities to their customers. But

132

in transactions in OTC securities, investment firms can act either as principal or as agent. Most frequently they act in the latter capacity. In this role, their broad experience with the complex off-board market is at the disposal of their clients. The experienced and professional commission house with its seasoned order traders will know which dealers and which cities provide the best markets in particular securities. While there is no legal requirement to do so, most brokers charge the same commission for OTC orders as they do for listed securities.

The investment firm may also act as dealer or principal in unlisted securities, which is one of the features distinguishing the OTC market from the various stock exchanges. The house acting as a dealer in a particular unlisted security to be sold OTC usually invests a portion of its capital in a "position," or inventory of stock, just as the specialist in exchange listed issues does. This inventory of stock is analogous to that maintained by any retail merchant and is laid in beforehand in anticipation of meeting the needs of his customers. The amount of profit realized by the dealer on a retail transaction is flexible and differs with the security and client. However, regulation and intense competition among dealers limit the degree of profit considerably.

Broker-dealer firms are usually categorized as "wholesale," "retail," or "integrated." The wholesaler makes a living by standing ready to buy or sell a security for his own account in dealing with other professionals. As a rule, he has few retail customers and depends on trading and position profits for a livelihood. The retailer has no market-making function and earns his profits from the commissions and markups on orders that come to him from his customers among the general public. The integrated firm (and most modern wire houses belong in this category) combines the wholesale-retail business under one roof. These integrated firms make markets to aid their registered representatives in retailing securities with which the firm is associated, or which are the subject of current or past recommendations. For instance, as the result of a favorable block purchase by the firm's trading department, its registered representatives will often benefit from having the stock for sale at a good price to its clients. In any case, in the integrated firms both the selling and trading arms work closely together, benefiting and supporting each other.

Because of the nature of the over-the-counter market, no focal point exists at which orders from public buyers and sellers can be matched and executed. The wholesaler-dealer becomes all-important in filling this need. For this purpose, he advertises his willingness to make a market in a given issue in the various inter-dealer publications. A wholesale market can be said to exist in a stock if a dealer stands ready to trade for his own account with other broker-dealers in amounts customarily traded in this security—this is called the "unit of trading." Whereas a single specialist, and only occasionally more than one, customarily makes a market in an issue listed on a stock exchange, there are some OTC stocks in which as many as thirty different broker-dealer firms compete in making a trading market.

The market-maker fills two important roles: He serves as a conduit through which buyer meets seller, and vice versa; and by selling long or short for his own account, the wholesaler contributes depth, stability, and continuity to markets. There is considerable variance, issue by issue, in the amount of professional participation, but in general, the more obscure and inactive a stock situation, the less likely it is that a professional would tie up his capital for prolonged periods of time by making a market.

Wholesale firms deriving the bulk of their income from inter-dealer transactions customarily base their decision on whether or not to trade a particular issue chiefly on the degree of activity in it. Other considerations, such as investment merit, or the quality of the sponsorship behind the security, are usually of only secondary concern. But integrated firms, which tend to treat their trading departments as an adjunct to their retail function, and the pure retail houses, approach matters differently. Their customers are individual investors—with all the responsibility that entails for the firms—rather than other professionals who are making presumably informed, rational decisions in trades. Integrated and retail firms must consider merit and quality of an issue, as well as current activity in it.

Profit margins on the wholesaler's big turnover are low, measured in small fractions. Some trades, hopefully the barest minimum, are transacted even, or at a loss. State transfer taxes, particularly in New York, weigh heavily on dealers and often turn a close trade into a loss. To ease this burden, a steadily increasing portion of business is being shifted to cities like Chicago and Los Angeles. A retailer's profit for a transaction is many times that of the wholesaler, but of course his volume is much smaller.

Persons responsible for committing their firms in transactions in the unlisted market are known as traders. The trader may be the owner of the firm, or an officer, the head of the trading department, or one of the specialists in that department. It is the function of the trader to see that all buying and selling transactions are concluded at the fairest price obtainable, and that an accurate and speedy report of the trade is made. Insofar as possible, this responsibility must be centralized with the trader. When inexperienced employees attempt to negotiate a trade for their firm, there are often unfortunate results, because of their lack of professionalism, or a failure to record the transaction properly, or simply because the entire transaction was unauthorized.

In the course of their working day, traders seldom come face to face with one another. Most buying and selling is done over wires without either side ever meeting or seeing the person with whom he deals. Quite commonly, traders who have dealt with one another for years and who work across the street from one another have never met. This reduction of the personal element poses problems, not only in the opportunities opened to an unscrupulous operator to pose as a representative of another firm in concluding a fraudulent trade, but because the slightest ethical departure wreaks havoc with a system founded completely on trust.

Crucial to the operation of the OTC market are the daily "sheets," published by the National Quotation Bureau, Inc. The "sheets" are the primary medium for the dissemination of price quotations among professionals in the OTC market, who use them to find and communicate a buying or selling interest in securities and to judge activity. They are available only to broker-dealers. In addition to their role in the securities market, the "sheets" provide the basis for computing certain taxes—notably death and estate taxes—and for the evaluation of loan collateral. While the bids and offers appearing in them may not be completely accurate in specifying the state of the market at the time of publication, quotations are supposed to be firm when submitted for publication. When a quotation is submitted by a broker-dealer, the latter is declaring that he is willing to trade on the market as quoted.

The sheets appear each day in three editions: The "pink sheets," or eastern section, are printed in New York and enjoy the largest circulation by far; the green sheets, or western section, are printed in Chicago; and finally, the white sheets, or Pacific coast section, are printed in San Francisco.

For at least half of the listings submitted by a subscriber, the bid or offering must include a price. If the broker-dealer simply is advertising a general interest, he may leave the price columns blank, or if he has an interest only in one side or the other, he may insert the letters "OW" (offer wanted), or "BW" (bid wanted). According to custom, any quotation inserted in the sheets indicates an interest in buying or selling at least one hundred shares, with an interest in fewer shares qualified as to the size of the interest.

The method by which a trade is effected is simple: The broker having a buy or sell order calls the dealers whose listings appear in the pink sheets and asks each for a market (a price). The broker finally trades with the dealer having the best bid or the cheapest offering. The dealer who gives a market in a particular stock has in effect made a unilateral offer to buy or sell at fixed prices. The broker requesting a market may now accept the offer by buying or selling, or he may reject the offer in several ways: by simply hanging up; or by counter bidding or counter offering to try to improve upon the original market, which has the effect of negating the existence of the first market. Brokers who attempt to do better, or customers who look for a bargain by bidding or offering in between the quoted prices thus run the risk of having the market move away from them, without the order being filled.

It is also quite possible to quote a market too often, so that by the time the broker calls back ready to do business, the dealer has become wary and either widens out his market or adjusts it up or down depending on which side he guesses the broker to be. Trying to save fractions by placing limit orders can also be a very expensive proposition for the broker or his customer. There is always a time lapse in securing a quote, getting an order, calling the market-makers with a bid or offer which is just shy of being good enough, and then calling the customer back to tell him his order could not be executed. If the limit is then raised to meet the original offering price, it is quite likely this new limit will again be short of the mark, since the dealers are now aware of the broker's intentions. At this point, the customer has several unhappy choices: raising his limit once more, canceling the order completely, or entering the order "open," or for the duration of the month, or some other period of time.

"A stock that's cheap at 40 is still cheap at 41," or "If you worry about paying a fraction too much for it, you shouldn't own it," or "If it's too high at 95, it's still a good sale at 94½" —these are just a few of the familiar old saws, all with a great deal of wisdom in them, which can be marshaled in favor of placing realistic limits on orders.

The value of limit orders to market-makers, and hence the limit orders' relative lack of real utility to investors, was well understood long ago. Every limit order properly worked is equivalent to a put and call option on which the broker may hang his dealings. Things being what they are, limit orders are usually filled only contrariwise to price swings, almost never within the market, and seldom in a sidewise, trendless market. In other words, a buy order placed at a price below the market will be filled only when the market has turned down, and is selling resoundingly below the limit order. A sell order placed above the market will be executed only when the market turns sharply upward.

Customers and registered representatives are often disturbed to find that a market has changed in the interim since a quote was given, and that their broker is now unable to execute an order based on the earlier price. Listed markets change, so why not the unlisted market? Just as on the stock exchanges, buying and selling interest tends to focus on individual stocks, so when one person is buying or selling, the odds are that others are competing and doing the same thing. All this activity moves the price and renders previous quotations obsolete.

Although it is common practice on the stock exchanges to request a "size" from the specialist in a stock, which means that the broker wishes the specialist to tell him the number of shares wanted and offered in a particular issue, it is much more difficult to find out the same information in the OTC market.

138

In point of fact, the broker who requests a size from a market-maker OTC is required to trade at least one unit in that issue, according to long-standing custom. Usually the broker requesting a size has a substantial order in hand, but before he discloses it, he would like to find out if the particular dealer is in a position to fill his order, or at least a major part of it.

Dealers will usually go to considerable length to accommodate what is known in the business as a "good call," which is an inquiry from a house or institution which deals with them on a continuing basis and has treated them fairly in the past. On the other hand, dealers are disinclined to make markets of any substance to their competitors for two reasons. First, the competitor may have seen an inquiry which he is unable to fill without assistance from the second dealer, who sees no enduring profit to himself in helping the first dealer satisfy the order. Second, in the long run, unless the market-maker is exceptionally talented, it is usually a money-losing proposition to trade consistently with one's competitors.

As a general proposition, OTC markets are either "firm" or "subject." When a dealer "makes a firm market," he is actually naming the prices at which he is willing to buy or sell, and once he has done so, he is obligated at that moment to trade at least the unit of trading at the price specified. A market is "subject" when the prices quoted are merely guides or indications of where the dealer thinks it may be possible for business to be done. The term "subject" is shorthand for "subject to confirmation," or "subject to customer approval," or even at times "subject" to a trader coming back from lunch. In any case, the market is conditional on some event that is beyond the dealer's power to influence at the moment.

Traders treat all markets as firm unless the market-maker immediately qualifies the market with words such as "subject," "workout," "indicated," "about," "quoted," "should work," "small," or any response which conveys to the inquirer that the other party is not in a position at that moment to buy or sell the equivalent of a trading unit, a hundred shares.

The OTC market has no central channel for the execution of orders, and thus "stop-loss" orders are generally not accepted. With multiple markets, it is quite possible for a stock or a bond to sell through the limit price at dealer A but not at dealer B or dealer C.

Short sales are sometimes effected for customers in unlisted markets, but only after the dangers of being "bought in" have been thoroughly clarified to the client. Dealers are very often short for their own account as a part of the trading business, but this type of short position is usually closed out fairly quickly or, in thinner, less active markets, the dealer short seller has warned the buying broker beforehand not to expect delivery within the automatic time. A broker will loan listed securities held by him to secure margin accounts to another broker to cover short sales made by the customers of the borrowing broker. But because Regulation T makes it unlawful for a broker to extend or maintain credit to or for a customer without collateral, or on any collateral other than securities listed on an exchange, or on certain exempt securities, OTC stocks are never held to secure margin accounts and are thus almost impossible to borrow. An unlisted short sale is thus very hazardous for a customer.

The foregoing description of the over-the-counter market should be helpful to any investor wishing to buy and sell unlisted securities. In all other respects, the rules pertaining to listed stocks that were developed in Chapters VI, VII, VIII, IX, and X apply to OTC stocks as well. The fluctuations in price level are apt to be more severe, and it is more difficult to get earnings projections, but the indications are that on average an investor can expect to do somewhat better with OTC than with listed stocks. At the present time, I do not have enough data to substantiate this hypothesis. But, almost certainly, on average you will not do worse than with listed stocks. Spectacular gains and hideous losses are more prevalent there than on the exchanges. Most readers of this book will probably want to stick with listed stocks where the probability of ruin is not so great, but for those investors with stout hearts, the OTC market is made to order.

Getting earnings forecasts on more than a handful of unlisted stocks is a problem. Two services that do give estimates on a few stocks are The Value Line Over-The-Counter Special Situations Service and the Growth Stock Outlook. In addition, the regular Value Line Investment Survey covers a few OTC stocks.

CHAPTER XII

HORSES, STOCKS, AND DEMOCRACY

No one of us is as smart as all of us.

THIS is the age of the expert. Pick any field, no matter how small and insignificant, and you will find an array of experts in it, people who know all that is known in that particular field. Most of us realize that not everybody can become expert in all matters where decisions must be made, and we are grateful that we do not have to decide which phosphor will give the brightest red in our color television set or what financial policies should be pursued to revive a faltering economy. We each have our own problems to worry about, and we leave it to the expert in other areas to judge the probability of success for any action undertaken there. However, in our democracy, we firmly believe that the people are the only ones who know the best interests of the people. We the people reserve the right to judge all results, both in the market place for commercial products and services and in the voting booth for political and economic policies. Through the financial and political power vested in our hands, we endeavor to select those experts best equipped to give us what we want. In this way, we believe, democracy makes use of the accumulated wisdom of all its people for the benefit of all.

Not everybody believes in this conception of democracy. In a dictatorship or absolute monarchy, it is thought that one man, supposedly more brilliant and capable than anyone else, can somehow rise above the massive problems that beset all of us, understand them, and take effective action toward their solution. In the Communist idea of democracy, only those who know the truth—the members of the Communist Party—have the right to decide what is best for the people. That too would be the case in any oligarchic system of government where a group of people, small in proportion to the total number in the whole state, runs the affairs of state. In each of these instances, there can be little doubt that the governing power sincerely believes that it promotes the advantage of all the people. What really results, however, is another story.

An interesting example of inner motives and later discordant consequences is given by the economist Milton Friedman, in *Harper's Magazine,* April 1967. He writes that the men who took charge of Japan in 1867 attached no special value to individual freedom or political liberty; on the contrary, they believed in aristocracy and political control by an elite. The men who took charge of India in 1948, on the other hand, were ardently devoted to political freedom, personal liberty, and democracy. Their aim was not national power, but improvement in the economic conditions of the masses. Yet it was the Japanese leaders who thoroughly dismantled the existing feudal structure and adopted a liberal economic policy that led to the widening of opportunities for the masses and great gains in personal liberty (up until their political ideas became the basis for tragic totalitarian excesses). It was the Indian leaders who adopted a collectivist economic policy that hamstrings their people with restrictions and continues to undermine individual freedom and political liberty.

143

Noble intentions and nice theories are not enough. At some point along the line, their correspondence with reality and their usefulness to society must be evaluated. Reality is a great deal more complex than most theories would lead one to believe, and it is a big mistake to take the two as synonymous. I remember in my younger years long arguments with proponents of Communism. They were quick to point out the defects of capitalism and extol the virtues of Communism, in theory. And they somehow could not understand when I demonstrated not only that the theory of capitalism held out just as much hope for the human race as any other economic theory, but that matters seldom work out according to theory.

Who then is to judge what is best? Who then will select the people best able to run things for the good of all? Who else but the public, acting as a whole! When the theory of public superiority, which is so vital to the idea of democracy, receives direct experimental confirmation from the fields of horse racing and common stock investments, it is a matter of no small import. Where there are no experiments, theories become merely matters of opinion and are subject to the fashion of the times. But in horse racing, we have shown that the betting public is superior to any one or number of individuals in determining the winning probabilities of the horses, and in choosing the horse most likely to succeed. In the stock market, we have shown that the investing public sets the price of each stock at such a level that a return greater than that from most other investments is available. The extension of the concept of public superiority to the political arena is not that great an extrapolation.

Although the results on horse betting and common stock investing represent the best scientific evidence available on this question of public superiority, other more speculative indications are not hard to find. An excellent case can be made for public superiority in recognizing great works of art, literature,

144

and music by contrasting the experts' critical response to these works at the time of their introduction, with the usually very rapid public acceptance of them. Indeed, the noted pianist and musical commentator, Abram Chasins, once devoted a whole radio program to demonstrating just this point in music. It is probably no accident that the last two world leaders, England and the United States, are democracies.

Dr. George Gallup believes that "the judgment of the people has often been wiser than the judgment of Congressmen or even of the experts," and he offers a rather striking example. One of the early issues on which he polled public opinion arose in 1935 "when Hitler was beginning to raise his ugly head and menace the world."

"The public was overwhelmingly in favor of building up our defenses; and 80% of the people wanted to build up our air force. But in 1935 and for the next few years, Congress was not willing to increase appropriations for defense, and the expert heads of the Army and Navy were telling us that air power would never be important in the next war.

"I believe that if the will of the people had been followed, if we had gone as far and as fast as they wanted us to go, there is even a chance there might not have been a World War II." *

Unwarranted notions of individual superiority in judgment over the public's ability to judge are not confined to horse racing and the stock market, but pervade all walks of life. Eric Hoffer, commenting in his book *The Temper of Our Time,* agrees. "The typical intellectual everywhere is convinced that the common people are unfit for liberty and self-goverment. . . . The intellectual in power seems to understand only the simple language of divisions, warships, bombers and missiles. . . . A ruling intelligentsia, whether in Europe, Asia or Africa,

---

* From a pamphlet, "Opinion Polls," published by the Center for the Study of Democratic Institutions founded by the Fund for the Republic, 1962.

treats the masses as raw material to be experimented on, proc-essed and wasted at will. . . . What the American intellectuals know about the American people is actually what they know about each other . . . they project upon America the infight-ing, mistrust, envy, malice, conformity, meagerness and stale-ness of their cliques and sects."

"A society that can afford freedom can also manage without a kept intelligentsia: it is vigorous enough to endure ceaseless harassment by the most articulate and perhaps the most gifted segment of the population. . . . Though there is no unequivocal evidence that the intellectual is at his creative best in a wholly free society, it is indubitable that his incorporation in, or close association with, a ruling elite sooner or later results in social and cultural stagnation."

For comparatively simple, narrow problems with few vari-ables, certainly the individual expert in a field is most com-petent, and there is little doubt that the public will quickly follow his lead. Once past narrow areas of specialization, how-ever, it is the public who seems best able to handle the prob-lems complicated enough to defy a rational approach. To many, this may be a most astounding and unexpected conclu-sion, the great wisdom of the people. Yet, we in America should not be too surprised, for the basic assumption of our democracy is that the people know best. Even our forefathers, the writers of the Constitution, had their doubts and tried to remove the selection of the President and the Senators from direct popular choice, an error long since rectified. Indeed, it would seem that the terms of our public officials should be shortened to allow more frequent judgment by the people. Of course, the people will make mistakes, but I think that they will make far fewer mistakes over a period of time than any single individual or small group of individuals.

Why is it, then, that democracy is such a rare phenomenon, that it does not take hold everywhere? Why are so many democracies fragile and fleeting? What conditions are necessary for it to flourish? Perhaps we can gain some understanding of these problems by observing carefully the simpler state of affairs at the race track, which may be considered as an isolated democratic world all to itself.

The most striking feature of public behavior at the race track is the spectacle of each person whole-heartedly and effectively acting in his own self-interest. Although this concept has been used many times in the past to account for public actions, it is indeed interesting to see it thrown into such sharp relief. The whole-hearted pursuit of a person's goal at the races is made possible by the simplicity of the goal—to select the right horses.

Not so clear is the much more complicated case of a political society. In established democracies, the situation is quite similar to that at the race track. Most people associate themselves with a political party to elect the representatives best able to look out for their interests. Such a choice is at best a compromise, however, since no party or candidate can possibly represent all of a person's varied interests. Many feel that the choice of party is meaningless and do not take any part in voting. In many countries, effective political parties do not exist at all, or, if they do, they take no real interest in the people's needs, with the consequence that the people are politically indifferent. Where indifference is of major proportions, whatever the reasons for it, there is small chance that democracy can work, just as there would be no horse racing without a variety of opinion. As Mark Twain said, "It were not best that we should all think alike; it is difference of opinion that makes horse races." And, probably, democracy, too.

The formulation of opinion by the people cannot occur in a vacuum and is, in reality, a very complex process. Let us again turn to the race track to see what happens there. As soon as we say the words "race track," we imply that there is an accepted order of things, that everybody plays by certain rules of the game, that there is an overall stability of the institution. Moreover, the rules encourage the formulation and diversity of opinion through the circulation of all information necessary for making a choice and through providing full public expression of all points of view. These things are accomplished first, by the availability of historical records on the horses, expert opinions, and all kinds of data pertaining to the races of the day, and second, by the "tote" board which exhibits all opinions in the form of odds against each horse winning. There are no social, economic, or political barriers placed in the way of anybody wishing to express an opinion—that is, to place a bet. Certain educational and economic levels are presumed however. Some knowledge of horses is essential for the public to make an informed opinion, and there must be capital available to make this opinion effective in the form of a bet. Finally, the race track has a wonderful way of reconciling all the different viewpoints simply by having a winner in each race. Over a period of time, there is something for everybody, the man who plays the favorites, the longshot player, the system player, and so on. Interestingly enough, the plurality of horse bettors, the favorite players, do best. There is a gradual decline in return for the smaller and smaller groups.

An almost identical analysis can be carried through by substituting stock market for race track and stocks for horses. For both the race track and the stock market, conditions are favorable for the emergence of public superiority.

Which of these same conditions are necessary for the establishment of a democracy? How many are sufficient? At present the answers to these questions are unknown. But one thing is clear. The acquiring of a stable democratic government must be a most difficult process, one that cannot happen overnight. If all or most of the above conditions that apply at the race track are necessary for the establishment of democracy, then

148

the achievement of democracy must involve, initially, another form of government. For until these conditions are satisfied, democracy cannot flourish, and if democracy does not flourish, few of these conditions can be satisfied. The establishment of democracy would be like pulling oneself up by one's own boot-straps, a process whose difficulty accounts for its rareness. Hopefully, the growth of democracy can be speeded by careful nurturing of all the conditions specified above by the well established democratic governments. In the long run, it seems likely that the non-democratic world will, as more and more of the prerequisites for the establishment of democracy are satisfied, become more and more like the democratic world. And, until that day arrives, the non-democratic world is un-likely ever to outdo the democratic world.

Appendices

THE PROBABILITY OF RUIN

THE formula for calculating the probability of ruin, q_z, when a gambler starts off with an initial capital, z, which he hopes to increase to an amount, a, when playing against an infinitely rich opponent always willing to play is as follows:

$$q_z = \frac{(q/p)^a - (q/p)^z}{(q/p)^a - 1}$$

where p is the probability of winning a dollar and q of losing a dollar on a single bet and p does not equal q. If p equals q

$$q_z = 1 - \frac{z}{a}.$$

The probability of success, p_z, is just

$$p_z = 1 - q_z.$$

A person hoping to win $1000 starting out with $10 and making one-dollar bets on the flip of a fair coin for which $p = q$ has a probability of doing so given by

$$p_z = \frac{z}{a} = \frac{10}{1000} = \frac{1}{100} = 1\%.$$

This means that he has a 1% chance of ending up with $1000 before losing his initial capital of $10.

153

PROBABILITY AT THE RACES

WE wish to determine first of all the winning probability assigned to a horse by the public. Suppose we start with a hypothetical race in which $100,000 is the total amount of money bet by the public on all the horses, with $50,000 bet to win on horse A, $25,000 on horse B, $10,000 on both horses C and D, and $5000 on horse E. The winning probability of a horse, in the opinion of the betting public, is given simply by the amount of money bet on that particular horse divided by the total amount of money bet on all the horses in the race. In the example, therefore, the public has assigned horse A the winning probability of 50,000/100,000, which equals ½ or 50%. Based on the information available at the start of the race, the public thinks that horse A has one chance in two of winning, a fifty-fifty chance. This means that if this race were repeated many times under exactly the same conditions, the public thinks horse A would win half the time. Horse B, according to the public, has a 25,000/100,000 or ¼ probability of winning—the public thinks that horse B would win one quarter of the time if this race were repeated many times. Similarly, horses C and D both have a 10,000/100,000 or 1/10 chance of winning and horse E a 5000/100,000 or 1/20 chance of winning. We may summarize all this in a concise formula for the winning probability of a horse,

$$p = \frac{m}{M} \tag{1}$$

where p is the winning probability assigned by the public, m is the amount of money bet by the public on the horse, and M is the total money bet in the pool.

Now the probabilities as such are not given on the totalizator or "tote" board at the track, which is the equivalent of the quote board in a stock house. Instead, there appear the odds on each horse which indicate the return or profit to be expected if a horse wins. Odds of two to one means that a bettor will have a two dollar profit for every dollar bet if the horse wins. Odds of four to five means a profit of four dollars for every five dollars bet. The amount of money in the pool available to be returned to the winners is obtained by subtracting from the total amount bet the money bet on the winning horse and the amount removed from the pool by the track. If this remaining money, which is the total profit to the winners, is divided by the money bet by the winners, there results the profit for each dollar bet, the odds. Putting all this into a concise formula, we have

$$o = \frac{M - m - fM}{m}. \tag{2}$$

Here, o is the odds figured to a dollar (the profit on each dollar bet), and f is the percentage take (the commission). Then fM is the amount of money removed from the pool by the track. In the above example, if the "take" is 15%, then 15% of $100,000, or $15,000, is removed from the win pool, leaving $85,000. If horse A won, the money bet on A is also subtracted, leaving $35,000, which is the amount to be returned as a profit to those people who bet on A. Since $50,000 was bet on A, only $35,000/$50,000 or 70¢ can be returned for each dollar bet on A. If horse B won, then the $25,000 bet on B is subtracted from the $85,000 left in the win pool, leaving $60,000 to be divided up among the people who bet on B, or $60,000/$25,000 which equals $2.40 for each dollar bet. Similarly, the dollar odds on horses C and D are $7.50, and on horse E, $16.00.

We need to establish a connection between the odds and the public's estimate of the winning probability of a horse. Equation

155

(2) may be written in the following form when each term in the numerator is divided by m,

$$o = \frac{M}{m} - 1 - \frac{fM}{m}.$$

From Equation (1), we see that $1/p = M/m$, and, substituting in the above equation, we obtain

$$o = \frac{1}{p} - 1 - \frac{f}{p}.$$

Rearranging, the desired result appears,

$$p = \frac{1-f}{o+1}. \tag{3}$$

Suppose we calculate some probabilities from the dollar odds when there is a 15% take. The numerator in Equation (3) is then equal to $1.00 - 0.15 = 0.85$. For dollar odds of \$0.70, $p = 0.85/1.70 = \frac{1}{2}$ or 50%. For dollar odds of \$2.40, $p = 0.85/3.40 = \frac{1}{4}$. For dollar odds at \$7.50, $p = 0.85/8.50 = 1/10$. For dollar odds of \$16.00, $p = 0.85/17.00 = 1/20$. The odds here correspond to the probabilities in the above example.

We have in Equation (3) the relationship between the payoff if a horse wins and what the public thinks of the horse at the start of the race. If the public assigns a winning probability of $1/10$ to a horse and the horse wins, the profit to those holding winning tickets is \$7.50 for every dollar bet. Now a winning probability of $1/10$ means that the public expects horses with this probability to win one race in ten. A person betting one dollar on this type of horse over ten races can expect to win once for a profit of \$7.50 and lose nine times for a loss of nine dollars, an overall loss of \$1.50 on the ten dollars risked. This \$1.50 loss on ten dollars is just the 15% commission extracted from the win pool by the track. More generally, we can use a formula that summarizes the above verbiage and gives the average return to be expected on one dollar bets

$$E = P \cdot o - (1 - P) \cdot 1.$$

156

P is the true probability of winning. Using the above example for some numbers, let us suppose that the public's probability $1/10$ equals the true probability and the odds are $7.50. Substituting, we have

$$E = \frac{1}{10} \times 7.50 - \frac{9}{10} \times 1 = -0.15 \text{ or } -15\cancel{c}.$$

On every dollar bet, we will lose $15\cancel{c}$, or 15% just as figured out above. In words, the formula says that the probability of winning o dollars minus the probability of losing one dollar (the original bet) is the net gain or loss arising from betting one dollar. Of course, the probabilities manifest themselves only after many bets, so that the expected return E is an average over many bets. For few bets, the changes in one's fortune can be tremendous. After all, if a bettor loses a bet, he loses 100% of the amount risked, and if he wins, he can win several hundred percent. For odds of $7.50, the winning percentage is 750%.

The formula for E can be written as follows:

$$E = P(o + 1) - 1$$

and if we substitute for $o + 1$ its value from Equation (3),

$$E = P \cdot \frac{1 - f}{p} - 1$$

or rewriting

$$E = \frac{1 - f}{p/P} - 1. \qquad (4)$$

If the public's winning probability for a horse equals the true probability, that is, if $P = p$, we have $E = -f$ and the game is unfavorable no matter what the odds or probability or the horse bet on. Over many bets, a gambler must lose a huge 15% of what he bets.

How realistic is the public's thinking of a horse's chances? Is it good enough to make the game unfavorable? For the game to be favorable, there must be a positive return for each dollar bet, or, putting it another way, E must be greater than zero. This can

157

happen only if p/P is less than $1 - f$ in Equation (4). Since $1 - f$ equals 0.85 for a 15% take, p/P must be less than 0.85, or the wining probability assigned by the public to a horse must be less than 85% of the true probability. Therefore, the public must make more than a 15% mistake in its probability estimates for the game to be favorable to an individual bettor.

Table I-B shows how the public takes a group of 93,011 horses and divides them up according to the public's estimate of their winning probabilities, which are obtained from the odds using Equation (3). The "true" winning probability is, to a very close approximation, just the winning percentage for horses in each odds grouping. Thus, the public assigned 5586 horses the odds of five to one and the corresponding winning probability of 13.2%. According to the public, 13.2% or 737 of these horses should have won. Actually, 686 or 12.3% of these horses won, and this number is taken as the true probability. In this way, the two sets of probabilities are compared in the table.

The last column gives the percentage loss to be expected if the same amount of money was bet on each horse in the group. If the public's estimates of the winning probabilities for all horses were exactly equal to the true probabilities, the percentage loss would always be 15%, just the "take." When the public underestimates the true winning probabilities, as it does for the shorter priced horses, the percentage loss is less than the 15% take. When the public overestimates the true winning probabilities, as it does for the longshots, the percentage loss is greater than 15%.

There are two things to be noticed. The first is the remarkable closeness of the true and public winning probabilities. Only for those groups of horses in the odds ranges less than five to two and greater than ten to one do the differences between the two probabilities fall outside the limits normally to be expected on the basis of chance fluctuations in the data. For those horses at odds between five to two and ten to one, there is no meaningful difference between the true and public probabilities. And, with the exception of the odds range 0.40–0.55, the public's winning probabilities are never more than 15% below the true probabilities, which is the condition necessary to make the game favorable. The public is

158

TABLE I-B. Comparison of true winning probabilities with the winning probabilities determined by the public.

Odds range	Public's probability	True probability	No. of horses and winners	% Loss
0.40–0.55	56.9%	71.3%	129–92	Profit
0.60–0.75	50.2	55.3	295–163	7.1%
0.80–0.95	44.9	51.3	470–241	3.8
1.00–1.15	40.6	47.0	615–289	2.4
1.20–1.35	37.1	40.3	789–318	8.1
1.40–1.55	34.1	37.9	874–331	6.1
1.60–1.75	31.5	35.5	954–339	4.8
1.80–1.95	29.3	30.9	1051–325	10.5
2.00–2.45	26.3	28.9	3223–933	6.5
2.50–2.95	22.8	23.0	3623–835	13.5
3.00–3.45	20.1	20.9	3807–797	11.0
3.50–3.95	18.0	18.6	3652–679	11.6
4.00–4.45	16.2	16.1	3296–532	15.3
4.50–4.95	14.8	15.5	3129–486	10.6
5.00–5.95	13.2	12.3	5586–686	20.1
6.00–6.95	11.4	11.0	5154–565	18.0
7.00–7.95	10.0	9.9	4665–460	16.4
8.00–8.95	9.0	8.2	3990–328	21.8
9.00–9.95	8.1	8.2	3617–295	14.7
10.00–14.95	6.5	6.0	12007–717	20.7
15.00–19.95	4.7	4.0	7041–284	26.4
20.00–99.95	2.5	1.4	25044–340	54.0
			93011–10035	

thus able to assign to groups of horses winning probabilities that turn out to be very accurate indeed. As already indicated, if such be the case, a bettor must lose 15¢ for each dollar bet, whether he be an expert on horses or a hunch-betting housewife. Any intelligent person might well pause and consider before placing a bet on the horses from here on.

Secondly, the public's estimate of the winning probabilities tends to underestimate the true probabilities more and more as the odds become shorter, making the shorter-priced horses better and better bets. Similarly, the longer-priced horses are too heavily played, resulting in greater and greater percentage losses of the amount bet. These statistics indicate a most important result: the

159

favorite, the horse on which is bet the most money, is the best bet at the race track. Obviously, the false lure of a big payoff has obscured the tremendous toll one must pay for betting longshots. Anyone betting horses at odds of twenty to one or longer may expect to lose over 50% of the amount bet, or 50¢ on every dollar bet over a period of time. That these results are not peculiar to this 10,000 race sample can be seen in the following summary in which the percentage losses of the amount bet (assuming flat bets) on the public favorites and the selections of leading public handicappers are compared in four different 5000 race samples.

Public favorites	10.8%	6.6%	9.2%	7.5%
Reigh Count	16.5	16.0	14.6	12.1
Armstrong	14.3	14.9	12.9	14.7
Sharpshooter	18.6	17.6	14.7	13.2
Hermis	15.0	15.5	18.7	14.8
Handicap	15.4	18.2	20.9	17.3
Sweep	15.9	18.5	19.0	16.4
Trackman	16.4	15.7	18.0	12.8

It is seen that the percentage lost of the amount bet on favorites is always well below the percentage takeout and well below that of the experts, whose losses cluster about 15%. This 15% loss indicates that the experts estimate the winning probabilities of their selections very accurately, and, therefore, they must lose the takeout percentage. Many excuses are offered for the relatively poor showing of the experts. But suffice it to say that the discrepancy between the performances of their selections and the public choices is so consistently great that there can be only one valid reason— the betting public is more expert. We have an extraordinary situation in which the public not only determines winning probabilities very accurately, but determines them in such a way that the public choices do best.

APPENDIX C

COMPOUND INTEREST

SUPPOSE XYZ Corporation is the stock picked at random. Its price on the randomly selected purchase date was $50 per share, and its price on the randomly selected sale date, which we will say occurred exactly three years later, was $150 per share. Over this period XYZ shares tripled in price. What is the percent return per annum compounded annually?

The way to handle this problem is usually learned in first year high school algebra, but for those readers who cannot remember that far back, I repeat the recipe. If you put $1 into a savings account which pays interest at the rate of 4% per year, your dollar will be worth 4¢ more or $1.04 one year later. Just multiply 1.00 by 0.04 to get the profit. During the second year, interest will be paid on $1.04 instead of $1.00. Multiplying 1.04 by 0.04 gives 0.0416 for your second year profit, and adding this amount to $1.04 gives $1.0816. Thus, at the end of the second year, your original dollar is worth $1.0816. In the third year, interest will be paid on $1.0816, and amounts to $0.043264. Adding this number to $1.0816 gives $1.124864 as the value of the original dollar after three years in the account. The compound interest formula summarizes this procedure concisely.

$$A = P (1 + r)^n$$

where P is the initial amount invested, r is the interest rate, n is the number of years the money is left in the account, and A is the final

161

total amount of money. For P equal to \$1, r equal to 4% or 0.04, and n equal to three

$$A = 1 (1 + 0.04)^3 = 1.124864$$

as above.

In the case of XYZ Corporation, we know everything but the interest rate r. A is \$150, P is \$50, and n is three.

$$150 = 50 (1 + r)^3.$$

Solving this equation for r using logarithms or tables yields a value of 0.44 or 44% for r. Thus XYZ Corporation yielded a return of 44% per year compounded annually over the three year period in question.

Suppose the stock of XYZ Corporation tripled in six months. Since six months is one-half of a year, the formula for determining r, the yearly interest rate, is, since n now equals ½

$$150 = 50 (1 + r)^{\frac{1}{2}}$$

and r equals 8.00 or 800%.

The interest rate needed to bring one's capital from \$1000 to \$100,000 in fifteen years is found from the following equation:

$$100,000 = 1000 (1 + r)^{15}$$

and $r = 0.36$ or 36%.

HOW TO EVALUATE A STOCK
SELECTION SYSTEM

SUPPOSE a person with a system selects n stocks that he says will do better than n other stocks over a certain period of time. At the end of the allotted time, calculate the percentage changes in price for each stock. Arrange each group of n stocks in order of decreasing percentage price change. Suppose k of the stocks in the system's favored group lead the corresponding stocks in the other group. How much chance would a person without a system, to whom all the $2n$ stocks would look the same, have of separating the $2n$ stocks into two groups such that there are k or more leads for one group over the other? If our systemless person has a high probability of doing so, the system's worth is doubtful. If he has a low probability of doing so, one can say with a high degree of confidence that the system is valid.

The formula for the probability of producing k or more leads for a group of n stocks over another group of n stocks, all stocks chosen at random from $2n$ stocks, is

$$p(k) = \frac{n - k + 1}{n + 1}.$$

As an example, the probability of getting fifteen leads for one group of fifteen stocks over another group of fifteen at random is $p(15)$. Substitution in the formula leads to

$$p(15) = \frac{15 - 15 + 1}{15 + 1} = \frac{1}{16}$$

163

which is about 6%. In other words, suppose a person picked from a group of thirty stocks fifteen that he said would outperform the other fifteen. If the fifteen so designated actually did outperform the other fifteen, there is still a chance that he was lucky and that he does not have a valid method of discrimination. For he has a 6% chance of doing this without any system by selecting at random from the thirty stocks.

It might be noted that averaging the percentage gains for the two groups of stocks and comparing the two average percentage gains is of doubtful significance. For it is quite possible that one outlandishly high or low result can greatly distort an average value for a moderate number of samples.

SHORT SELLING

ORDINARILY, a person buys a stock, hoping it will go up in price, and sells on some later date. During the period in which he owns the stock, he is said to be "long" of the stock. However, the stock exchanges make it possible to reverse this procedure. A person may sell a stock that he does not own, hoping it will go down in price, and buy it back at a later time. During the period between these two times, he is said to be "short" of the stock, and the selling process is known as selling short. If the stock goes down after selling short, the speculator can buy it back at a lower price. He therefore makes a profit which is the difference between the selling price and the buying price, minus commissions. If the stock goes up after selling short and he buys it back at a higher price, he has a loss. When a stock is bought back after a short sale, the short sale is said to be "covered."

What actually goes on is this. If you tell your broker to sell 100 shares of General Motors short, he will borrow the shares from some other investor and sell them. Your account is then credited with the proceeds from the sale. When you cover, the stock is returned to its owner. While you are short, you must pay the owner of the shares any dividends that accrue. When selling short, it is necessary to put up with your broker a sum of money that depends on the margin rates in existence at the time. If the margin requirement is 70%, you must put up 70% of the selling price of the stock.

RELATION BETWEEN PRICE CHANGES, EARNINGS CHANGES, AND PRICE-TO-EARNINGS RATIO CHANGES

IF P is the price of a stock, E the earnings per share, and R the price-to-earnings ratio, the following equation holds.

$$P = E \cdot R$$

To determine how changes in these quantities are related to each other, we make use of the differential calculus and differentiate this equation, obtaining a relation between a change in price and changes in earnings and price-to-earnings ratios.

$$\Delta P = R \Delta E + E \Delta R$$

ΔP is the change in price corresponding to a change in earnings per share, ΔE, and a change in the price-to-earnings ratio ΔR. If each term in this equation is divided by P, which equals ER, we have the important equation

$$\frac{\Delta P}{P} = \frac{\Delta E}{E} + \frac{\Delta R}{R}.$$

The percentage change in price equals the percentage change in earnings plus the percentage change in price-to-earnings ratio. If the price-to-earnings ratio remains constant, $\Delta R = 0$ and any price change in a stock is determined solely by the change in earnings.

$$\frac{\Delta P}{P} = \frac{\Delta E}{E}.$$

THE "PROPER" PRICE-TO-EARNINGS RATIO FOR A STOCK

A COMPANY earned $1.00 per share in its last fiscal year and sells at $10.00 per share. We wish to determine whether or not this is the proper price to pay for the company's stock.

To begin, a projection of the company's earnings over some period of time into the future must be made. Based on the available information, the earnings are expected to grow at a 5% annual rate for the next ten years. Using the compound interest formula, the earnings ten years from now may be determined.

$$E = E_0 (1 + g)^{10}$$

where E is the earnings expected in ten years, E_0 is last year's earnings of $1.00 per share, and g is the assumed growth rate in earnings. Here, g equals 5%, or 0.05. Performing the calculation, we arrive at earnings ten years from now of $1.63 per share.

$$E = \$1.00 (1 + 0.05)^{10} = \$1.63$$

Next, we must decide what multiple on these earnings will be applied by the stock market ten years from now so as to determine the price of the stock then. If the same multiple that exists at present, ten times, is assumed, the price of the stock in ten years will be $16.30 per share.

Finally, we must determine what rate of return per annum on the original investment represents a fair return. If 9% per year is decided on, we can use the compound interest formula again to find out what present price, compounded annually at 9% for ten years, will transform into $16.30. If P_0 is this present price per share,

$$P_0 (1 + 0.09)^{10} = \$16.30$$

and solving, $P_0 = \$6.875$. This price represents the "proper" value of the stock, based on the assumptions made, so the present market price of $10.00 per share makes the stock overpriced.

The whole procedure may be compressed into one inclusive formula for the present "proper" price to pay for a stock.

$$P_0 = \frac{R E_0 (1 + g)^n}{(1 + r)^n}$$

where R is the price-to-earnings ratio applied to the company's earnings by the future stock market n years in the future, g is the assumed growth rate per year in earnings, and r is the rate at which future value is discounted back to the present.

The "proper" present price-to-earnings ratio for a stock, R_0, is obtained by dividing through by E_0.

$$R_0 = \frac{P_0}{E_0} = \frac{R (1 + g)^n}{(1 + r)^n}$$

Let us apply this formula to International Business Machines. In 1967, IBM earned $5.00 per share and let us forecast a 15% growth rate in earnings for the next ten years. If we assume that the earnings ten years from now will be capitalized at forty times and that future value will be discounted at 9%, we arrive at

$$R_0 = \frac{40 (1 + 0.15)^{10}}{(1 + 0.09)^{10}} = 67.5$$

as the "proper" present price-to-earnings ratio for IBM. The "proper" present price to pay for IBM is 67.5 times $5.00, the present earnings per share, or $337.50 per share. This figure is close to the present actual price.

INDEX

INDEX

172

174